MYSTICISM
THE PSYCHOLOGY OF LOVE

SHARAM

WITH
SHAHED HARRIS

TALIA

MYSTICISM:
THE PSYCHOLOGY OF LOVE
SHARAM

POETRY BY: SHAHED HARRIS
PAPERBACK 1ST EDITION
PUBLISHED IN 2012 BY:

TALIA

TALIA, FRIENDS OF EXISTENCE, INC.
WEBSITE: WWW.TALIAFRIENDS.ORG
EMAIL: TALIA@TALIAFRIENDS.ORG

COPYRIGHT © 2012 BY TALIA, FRIENDS OF EXISTENCE, INC.
ISBN 978-0-9839873-2-1

ALL RIGHTS RESERVED.

NO PART OF THIS BOOK MAY BE REPRODUCED, STORED IN A RETRIEVAL SYSTEM, OR TRANSMITTED IN ANY FORM OR BY ANY MEANS, ELECTRONIC, MECHANICAL, PHOTOCOPYING, RECORDING OR OTHERWISE, WITHOUT THE PRIOR WRITTEN PERMISSION OF THE PUBLISHER.

COVER ART: SHARAM
PAINTINGS & ART: ALL PAINTINGS BY SHARAM,
EXCEPT: MONA (P.168 P.215), NAFISEH (P.5, P.232)

The Paintings

Sharam's paintings have been added to the book to bring more joy and peace to your reading. Sharam was never taught to paint. One day he just picked up a brush, started painting, and Existence came through. Like Zen paintings, his paintings are very simple. The figures, mainly trees and flowers, are there to emphasize the emptiness of the blank page behind them.

The Glossary

While reading, if you come across a mystical concept you are unfamiliar with, there is a glossary at the end of the book for reference.

"If the ego wins, we lose. If we win, the ego loses."

–Sharam

CONTENTS

Introduction xv
Wanting Attention 3
Cheerleader for the Soul 5
Daily Path 8
Blame 9
Definition of Escape 17
The Tao of Talent 21
Totality for Transformation 25
Balance 26
The Positive Way 27
Singing in the Shower 29
Making a Conscious Choice 31
Gentle Controlling 33
Drop the Sugar Coating! 34
Throw the Anger Out 37
Assertiveness Gives Me Juice! 39
Acceptance Is Everything 40
Negativity Is Totally Optional 42
Worrying Means "I Am Important" 45
Bad and Good 49
Connection with Existence 52
Finding Your Center 53
The Bitch 55
On Expressing 57
Inferiority Leads to Superiority 61
Taking Responsibility 63
Passivity Comes from Fear 69
Anxiety Is Good 73

Wrong Is Right, Right Is Right	76
Don't Be Greedy	77
Crying Cleanses Karma	79
Love and Freedom	80
Love and Freedom Continued	83
Existential Interference	85
The Diamond in the Rough	87
Everything Has Spiritual Value	93
The Subtlety of Lying	95
I Deserve	97
Seven Candles	99
Our Partner as Our Unconscious	101
What Is Anger?	105
Detoxing Instead of Retoxing	107
Say "Cheese"	109
Everything Is Perfect	111
The Good and Bad of Guilt	115
Energy, the Mind, and the Moment	117
The Peacemaker	119
Room for Improvement	123
Self-worth	125
Acceptance	127
The New Apartment	131
Who Is Responsible for What?	133
If the Ego Wins, We Lose	134
Snoring	135
Thinking Versus Awareness	137
Periods, Self-confidence, and Tooting Your Own Horn	141
Worry and Seizures	145
Inner Dialogues	149
Resist Not	151
Heaven or Earth	153
The Table	157

Ready To Be Whatever You Want Me To Be	161
Oh Yes You Do Need It!	165
Bypass the Ego with Subtlety	169
Tool Kits	171
Becoming One with Negativity	173
Gaining Maturity?	177
Sittings	178
The Path of Love and the Path of Meditation	179
Cement	181
Resistance	182
Repeating Himself	184
The Machine vs. the Moment	185
Any Moment	191
Pathways to the Emotional Body	193
Poverty of the Mind	197
Ego as Desire	201
The Best Sitting of Rabia's Life	203
Doubt: Taking a Few Steps Back To Leap Forward	209
Spiritual Root Canal	213
Feeling Included	216
We Are Not Here To Live, We Are Here To Grow	217
The Chamber	219
Desiring	223
Two Birds	226
The Mathematics of Love	231
The Three Steps out of Passivity	233
I Am Better	235
Expectations	239
Negativity and Ego	243
The Ego Is Absolutely Great!	247
The Beauty of Bothering People and Being Bothered	249
Responsibility Revisited	251
Male Energy	257

Transformation Means Acceptance	259
The Way of the Moment	261
Trust	263
The Mechanics of Watching	269
Glossary	271

MY CIRCLE

Believe it or not there is something I see
I have a circle of friends who are intimate with me
Sometimes we think we are different
But now I know we're not
Thrown together for a reason
Into Master's pot.

You see:

I have an issue that I know not
Or maybe I have an inkling
But don't want to be put on the spot
So God gives me Roxana, or Sophie
Or even Baba ... why not.
I can see it in them
Clear as a bell
Sometimes with compassion
Sometimes giving hell.

Or there's days I've lost my courage,
But Rabia's is intact
Boldly sharing what I cannot
Healing both our wounds is Master's pact.
Other times I feel so ugly
Better leave, just be alone
Then Aziz gives me a hugly
Melting heart of stone.

In so doing we come closer
Growing faster every day
Dropping fear and self protection
Ruining ego's play.
I love you and I love you
I love you even more
And because you all love me so much
Myself I less abhor.

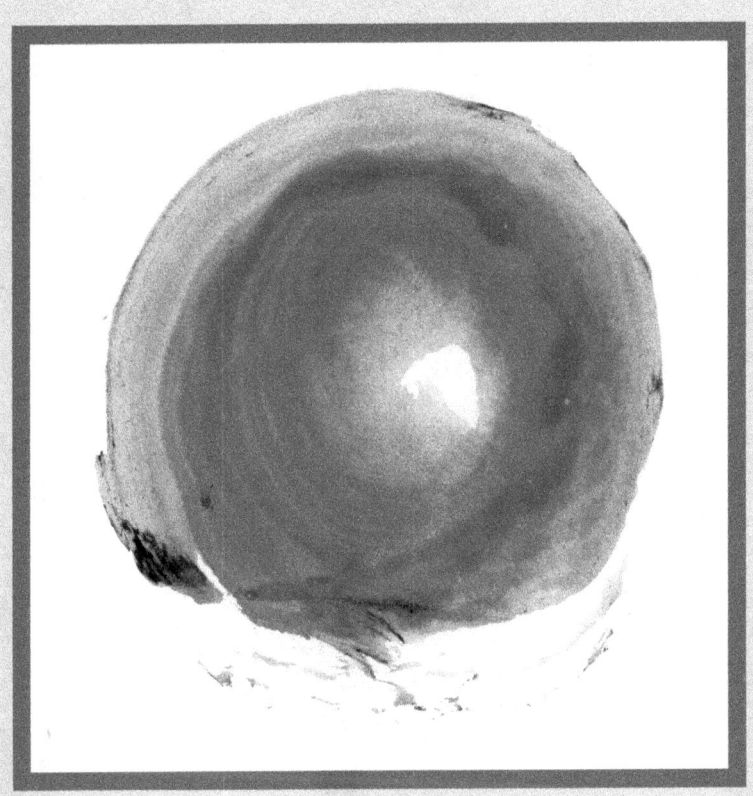

INTRODUCTION

MYSTICISM has long been a part of Eastern traditions like Buddhism and Hinduism, as well as a part of Middle Eastern and even Native American traditions. It has been much slower to catch on in an industrialized West that prides itself on individualism, productivity, and the power of the mind over that of the heart. However, a hunger for wisdom and more importantly the love that comes with this wisdom, is growing exponentially here. The West with all its technology, wealth, and abundance is struggling with greater and more meaningless violence, an environment in trouble, youth who turn increasingly to drugs and alcohol, and a general lack of satisfaction in life and love. Old and young are searching for a deeper meaning in their lives. Religion has laid the groundwork to prepare us for even deeper work, the search for the soul and the experience of oneness with all things.

Sharam

Sharam was born into the world of mysticism. His life has been filled with mystical experiences, experiences that even at a young age marked him as someone bound for an extraordinary life. His parents raised him in the Sufi faith, but he has worked with spiritual teachers from many different paths throughout his life.

Although we refer to Sharam as "our teacher," he does not consider himself to be one. He says, "I do not teach. It is more like a river.... Whoever is thirsty will drink from it." In seeking other terms to describe the essence of Sharam, we considered words like master, guide, spiritually advanced person, and others. Finally we agreed on the simplicity of the word mystic, someone who understands and connects with the subtle energies of Existence.

Anyone spending time with Sharam will begin to see miracles happening around him all the time, big and small, but when asked for "cool" mystical stories to introduce him to readers and publishers, he replied, "It is not because of anything I do that these miracles happen. It is because the energy of my master travels with me, not because I will it." When a person stands deep within his inner self, he becomes a great miracle for those who are still suffering. We have seen Sharam open the hearts of many men and women. These are the real miracles.

Because a mystic has conquered his own ego, his eyes are clear to catch the ego of others and work with them lovingly. Many people can see the egos of others, but usually we react to what we see. We mix up our ego with theirs. When our ego becomes involved, all clarity is lost. Why is this? Because we are so closely identified with our own ego, it is very hard for us to see it clearly. Staying uninvolved, or keeping one's own ego out of the equation, is a quality that is needed in order to help others.

In working with his students, Sharam's tools are love, humor, wisdom classes, sittings, breathing exercises and meditation. Like that of all mystics, Sharam's work heads in unexpected directions, challenging belief systems, behaviors, conditionings, and even the morality that ego depends upon to keep us from our real selves. He uses a wisdom that comes from beyond the mind to conquer the enemy of our soul. He constantly reminds us that he is at war with our enemy, our ego, the source of all our misery, not us. "It's a dirty job," he says, chuckling, "but someone's got to do it."

*"In 1987, I walked into a classroom where
I was teaching and I wrote on the board,
'Almost everything we know
is one hundred eighty degrees
from what the reality is.'
All my life since then has been focused on
learning and sharing about this truth.
It has been a great journey.
Life becomes so exciting, so free,
when you discover that the reality of life is
actually the reverse of what we've been taught.
The ego might not like it,
but if you work beyond the ego,
life becomes so fun."*

–Sharam

The One Hundred Eighty-Degree Rule

The focus of *Mysticism: The Psychology of Love*, and a great deal of Sharam's work with his students, revolves around what he calls sittings. These are times when we sit in front of him, one at a time, and share issues we are having either in the world or in our spiritual work. In these sittings, Sharam often talks about the One Hundred Eighty-Degree Rule, the idea that the rules, laws or ideals of society often directly conflict with, or are one hundred eighty degrees from, what he calls the Laws of the Universe, of Existence, or more simply put, the laws of love. Most of us are well-versed in the laws of society and have been from a young age: things like a belief in good and bad, more is better, a good education is the key to success, success is important, anger is bad, learn from the past, plan for the future, be on time—the list goes on and on. The difficulty is that these rules, and subsequently our egos and minds, have developed from a misunderstanding of the reality of Existence.

With Sharam, we learn the ways and means of Existence, of love. For example, we discover that ultimately, there is no good and bad. Everything is God and God is only love. We learn that believing in a concept like good and bad, although important for children, as adults just tends to fuel feelings of inferiority or superiority, and guilt. This, then, breeds comparison, competition, and a desire to be different from who we are, which immediately throws us into misery and closes our hearts to ourselves and others. As students sit in front of Sharam and share, we see how these deeply held societal beliefs, passed down through the generations, fuel our misery, and how simple understandings of the ways of Existence can immediately transform this same misery into acceptance, joy, and gratitude.

Transformation

Sitting with a mystic is a much greater phenomenon than just talking about our issues. When we sit in front of him, a transformation happens, and that transformation goes beyond the mind. It reaches the soul. Whether the transformation results from a deeper understanding of wisdom shared, or from a smile, a look, or a breathing exercise the student lets go and surrenders to the energy of Existence. In these moments, a deep connection occurs, a moment of oneness between the teacher and the student. This is what Sharam calls a transformation—when the student jumps above the poles of an issue such as good/bad, male/female, love/hate, right/wrong, and comes to acceptance. It is when he or she jumps out of the ego and simply connects with the teacher from a place of joy and surrender (egolessness).

A transformation is almost like a mini-enlightenment, a taste of where we are headed. The ego does come back until we reach the ultimate enlightenment, but each transformation accumulates like money deposited in the bank. The more they accumulate, the richer our connection with the soul becomes and the weaker the hold of the ego upon us. The more we are flexible and ready to let go of our cemented conditionings, the more easily transformation happens for us. The more we resist and are not willing to let Existence enter us, the less we transform. So, basically, transformation means replacing our cemented conditionings with Existence's laws, and how much we transform depends on the degree to which we are open or the degree to which we resist.

Although Sharam's work with each student is tailored to that student, there are nonetheless universal truths shared within each sitting. These universal truths became the inspiration for this book. We invite you to read *Mysticism: The Psychology of Love* with an open heart. Sharam's being walks within these pages. Each sitting is complete within itself. Whether you choose to read this book cover-to-cover or to just open it anywhere and let Existence choose its message for you, the essence of the book comes through.

The Sittings

WANTING ATTENTION

SHARAM: You talk about attention. When we are a kid, we want to get the attention of other people by being funny and saying smart things. Then we get older and the element of sex comes in and we want to get attention by being sexy or being pretty. We want to get attention from the opposite sex. So life is about getting attention and we have to understand why. Why is it all about getting attention? Because we think, deep inside, that we are not good enough. If we get the attention of other people, it's validation that we are good. If we really think we are good enough, it doesn't matter if we get attention or not. So, it is just that thing again of bad and good. I'm not good enough, so therefore, attention makes me feel great. And it's not just out there, even here *(with Sharam)*, without attention from me, you may fall apart because you think, "Oh, Sharam doesn't give me attention because I am not good enough." We just have to understand that it all has to do with how we feel about ourselves.

CHEERLEADER FOR THE SOUL

Livia is a seventy year old woman who has been working with Sharam for about five years now. In this sitting, she told Sharam how thankful she is for him and the work they are doing together, and that she wants to become even more dedicated in her work with him.

SHARAM: We keep ourselves busy all the time to avoid the mind going deeper into a lot of layers of pain. But we want to pass these layers; we want to get to the source. By sitting here, we are telling Existence we really want to get to the source. All of you are. I am sitting here, and I'm so glad I declared to Existence, too. We have all experienced ups and downs. When you get older, if you don't do anything about it, you will experience much worse pain, loneliness and nostalgia.

So we want to pass through all this and get to the source, which is pure ecstasy for eternity. But what does it mean to go to the source and how do we get there?

Going to the source basically means putting the ego aside, or getting the ego out from between our soul and what is happening in the moment. It means that your ego doesn't interfere. There are two paths to get there.

One is the path of meditation, the path of effort. If you give some information to the brain, you have knowledge. If some information goes to the heart, you have love. If information goes to the soul, you have meditation.

So:
> **mind** = knowledge;
> **heart** = love;
> **soul** = meditation.

Here, you have gone to the very essence of Existence with meditation and breathing exercises. How? When you do breathing exercises, all of a sudden, the soul pops up, comes to the surface, and meditation happens. So by meditating, we are allowing the soul to come out, to expand, and when that expansion happens, the ego steps aside. The more we meditate, the more the ego steps aside until eventually, it steps aside for good.

But we can also put the ego aside consciously and expand. In the path of love we catch the ego, see it in action. When we catch it, or someone else catches it for us, and we do not defend ourselves, we expand right away. The ego steps aside right away. The path of love is also called the path of trusting Existence. Trusting that everything that is happening is just as it should be, just as Existence wants and needs it to be. We watch ourselves, our egos, not to change them, but to be aware of ourselves and our motivations. It is one perfect way to reach enlightenment.

In the millions of years on Earth, there are just these two paths: the path of love that comes from trust, and the path of meditation, a very slow path.

Besides meditation there is opening yourself, understanding what is happening in the moment. Opening oneself belongs in both paths. Now, in the twenty-first century, with the fast-paced lives we live and the complicated minds that we have, it is important to deal with the mind directly. That's why we have sittings, so you can understand where you are coming from and where you are going. I confront the arguments of the mind head on to help you go deeper. The wisdom classes where I read are pure fun.

My job is to be your cheerleader, to cheer you up. So I will bring my pompoms.

DAILY PATH

The next three sittings happened as one sitting, but they are divided up by subject matter for clarity's sake.

CHRIS: It seems like I'm not on either the path of meditation or the path of love. I couldn't make myself get up this morning at 6:00 a.m. for exercises.

SHARAM: The day you can't make yourself get up and do your meditation, that day you are on the path of love. The day you do your meditation, that day is the day you are on the path of meditation. It's that simple.

BLAME

CHRIS: Right now, I feel total resistance. You said that in our subconscious we blame others, but I feel I do it consciously. I don't stop it. I am aware of it, but it doesn't seem to change.

SHARAM: Why do you want to change it?

CHRIS: You told us, when you blame, you close yourself.

SHARAM: Yes, when you blame, you close yourself. When you close yourself, you blame. It's a vicious circle.

CHRIS: It seems like when I'm in negativity, all I do is blame, I defend, and I don't take responsibility.

SHARAM: It's this way with everyone. When there is too much pressure, we blame other people. More pressure, more blame. But, when you verbalize it, like you just did by saying "I blame," then something has changed already. Right now, there is a change, but the change is very subtle. The mind doesn't grasp it. Just right now when you said, "I blame others," you stopped blaming others because you verbalized it. You took responsibility. Now you see it doesn't make sense to blame others. As soon as we take responsibility, we are open. We feel love. The mind cannot understand this concept. Only the heart can. I understood what you said because of the heart. Right now, you do feel love. Just this moment. The mind will maybe catch on in a couple of minutes, but right now, the feeling of love has started.

CHRIS: The blame, if it is that bad in the conscious, is it *really* bad in the subconscious?

SHARAM: It's a very subtle thing to understand the subconscious. Subconscious doesn't have language. It works with pictures. Is it that bad? No, not really. We have been taught that we are so good and everyone else has a problem, one picture. Also, we have been taught that we are so bad, and everybody else is so good, another picture. So, all these pictures are there. It just depends on which picture comes up in the subconscious at the moment and slips into the conscious, but both pictures are there.

We want to understand. What is understanding? Understanding means that through the conscious mind, that knows language, we change the subconscious. Through understanding, we change language to a picture and print it into the subconscious. For example, I tell you there is no good or bad. You picture that and then you print it into your subconscious. In your subconscious now there is a picture that there is no good, there is no bad. When we hear the word good, there is a cross on it with a red line and circle around it. No good. When we hear the word bad, also there is a cross on it with a red line and circle around it. Like traffic signs. There are many things in the subconscious, but that is good because they are helping us grow.

"When we stay centered, we take responsibility for our experiences. The result is that we don't repress. We express and heal. When we blame, we throw the responsibility on others, which requires us to repress the parts of ourselves that we don't want to see or accept."

–Sharam

RIGHT HAND

Master asks,
"When your right hand
Slaps your left,
Do you get angry at it?"

Do you rail at it?
Lose sleep planning your revenge?
Do you put it behind your back
While talking about it
To a friend
Convincing them
What a jerk
It is?
"Can you believe it could be so cruel?"

Do you resist getting out of bed
Every morning
For fear you may bump into
Mr. Right Hand
While brushing your teeth?

Will you align yourself with only
The left hands of the world
And soundly reject
"Rights"
As the oppressors of society?

Will you keep your gaze
Focused above
The waist of society
In order
To avoid hands altogether?

But what about basketball games,
Hailing cabs,
Warm waves of hello
Scratching noses,
Eating,
Hugs
…?

You could stay home
Locked in your house
With only left hands you know,
Refusing invitations
To parties, reunions,
To Master and meditations,

But what of visitors?
"Is that a right hand knocking or a left."
And writing?
Will you write with only your left hand
Regardless of how childish that writing appears,
How illegible?

"Gosh," I cry.
"I'll probably cripple myself
Right into orthopedic shoes
Keeping that evil right hand and
The traitorous arm that carries it
Behind my back
And out of sight."

What about a glove?
A glove might work.
The King of Pop's revenge,
Pink with velvet flowers
Faux fur cuff, sequins?
That might work.
Hmm.

"I'm sorry,
What was the question again?"
Oh yeah,
When my right hand slaps my left hand
Do I get angry at it?

"No.
Of course not.
What are you nuts?
I mean my left and my right
Are both a part of me.
We are one.
It was probably just swatting at something
Trying to bite me anyways."

DEFINITION OF ESCAPE

HOME

I feel tight in my chest
Cause it isn't my time,
Should I go? Should I go?
Everyone belongs,
Everyone responds,
But
I feel weird,
Exposed,
Raw and naked
Holding a pose,
While
Others walk by
Living their lives,
Where am I?

ANN: I am going through menopause. I have symptoms such as sudden tears and extreme highs and lows. Also, I tend to cry a lot. Do these hormonal highs and lows and all this crying help my growth?

SHARAM: There are two kinds of crying. The first is the one which is not the kind where you cleanse. There is no outburst. You just make your eyes wet. There is no pumping or cleansing of karma. It is more like you are hiding behind sorrow or feeling sorry for yourself. It is a "no value" cry. But when you cry with totality, then things come out. There is value in that cry.

So, there are two kinds of crying. One is feeling sorry for yourself—you fall into your emotional body because you don't want to look at yourself—and the other one has totality. If there is totality in whatever you do, there is value. When you really cry, when you go deeper into the cry, there is an explosion in the emotional body and you come out of it automatically.

ANN: I feel like these mood swings make everyone hate me. What is the best way to handle it when I fall into these tears and emotional highs and lows? Is it to go outside? Or leave?

SHARAM: Does that help you when you go outside?

ANN: It helps everybody else.

SHARAM: If it helps you, then it helps everybody else too, so let's see how we can get help. The first thing is, let's not worry about other people for now. When you go outside, if it is escape, not only does it not help you, but it doesn't really help others either. Does it help you to go outside?

ANN: It gives me space. I can go through this and not feel I have to put on a face. It is a space I can go to, so that if I want to cry, or have a long face, or not interact socially, I can.

SHARAM: So it does help. What is escape? It means you do something you don't like to do, and that is escaping. If you do something and you like it, then it is not escaping anymore. If you do something with some understanding, then it is not escape. If you go out there and you want the space and the space helps you, you can cry, it is perfect. It is not escaping.

We learned the definition of escape. It means you do something that you think is wrong, and you don't like it, and that becomes escape. For example, some people smoke, or drink, or eat something they think they shouldn't.

ANN: Are just going through *(menopausal)* highs and lows in themselves helping me spiritually?

SHARAM: You go high and low in your emotions. It doesn't matter if it is because of menopause or you have a fight or someone looks at you the wrong way. It doesn't matter why. You go high and low and then you come and sit here and you express yourself and you learn a few things. Going high and low not only helps you understand something, but also, each time you go high and low, you go a little bit higher. Just by itself. So, you are gradually growing spiritually, just by going high and low. You go to two opposite poles, high and low. Every time we go to opposite poles, when we return, we have expanded our horizons just a little bit. Maybe we don't like to go to the lows, but for the sake of expanding our horizons, it is very useful.

When reviewing this sitting for the book, Sharam added this.

SHARAM: Crying in the group, with your teacher, is so healing. When you cry here, in the group, it is more effective; it is cleansing and healing. When you cry alone, you might feel sorry for yourself. You think, "I am here all alone. Nobody cares." So, in a way, you could harm yourself, making karma instead if cleansing it.

THE TAO OF TALENT

SHARAM: Nothing I do is really a talent. When I put my brush on a paper, all of a sudden it happens. Many things I paint are not nice. I rip them up and throw them away. Why are they not nice? Because we are conditioned that certain things are nice. These kinds are not nice. It is because of our conditioning. But Existence doesn't have that conditioning.

KATE: How does my mind, that has been conditioned that I need to have a talent, let go of that conditioning? I see I am wasting all of my energy and time inside, struggling with this.

SHARAM: There is something in you that says, "I need to be liked. They need to love me, and I need to have a talent so they like me." So, all the need to have a talent is that you believe you need to have something special so people will love you. But if you happen to become enlightened, you don't care about love from others and others will love you anyway. As long as we want others to love us, just that wanting becomes a barrier, and they won't. The wanting becomes expectation. But as soon as we don't care about their love and we don't care about talent any more, there will be so much energy available that other people will be drawn to you like a magnet. They will be drawn to you because of the energy that you are not wasting on worrying.

As a child, they told us that our whole worth comes from other people liking us, and we believed in it. They said, "Sit very nicely and put your hand like this. Be nice so people will like you and they will respect you. Don't run like a kid; be a lady." They trained you that you need to be a certain way so people will like you. That's the only value you learned from childhood—you need to be liked.

Also from childhood, we have been told over and over that we need to have a talent or an education. Those are the most important things. This becomes deep-rooted in you and all your life you are always thinking about this, that I need to have a talent or higher education. If you get these, you will have self confidence. If you don't get these, you will always feel that you are not good enough. So, in a sense these conditionings become deep wounds. On this condition, you are good. On this condition, you are worthwhile. Otherwise you are not good. This is damaging to the Being. The Being is excellent, the highest, but we become totally focused on certain conditionings or wounds. If we are not so worried about being talented or not talented, if we say whatever I am is great, then we have a lot of energy that is not going to the wound. We will be free. We can even use that energy to become educated, become talented, and to heal that wound, if we want.

Usually the egos of people that have talent, but are not wise, get really big. They misuse their talent. They go to drugs or they have a lot of problems. You don't have the problems many famous people have. You are worry-free. Who wants the talent when it will cause you to worry all your life about so many things, unless you have wisdom to go along with that talent?

The things they taught us were the wrong things. They should have said, "Meditate." Instead, they said, "Be nice, don't swear, work hard, win." From childhood, you thought the only thing that is worthwhile in the whole world is for them to like you. Nothing else is valuable.

What I do is constantly grab a hammer and hit your conditionings on the head.

LONE FISH
The Tao of Talent

A lone fish breaks the surface of glassy ocean
Looking down through his reflection
To the beautiful, ever undulating, iridescent mass
Of his fellows.
Stunned by the beauty of their ordinariness,
He arches ecstatically through the air
And disappears.

TOTALITY FOR TRANSFORMATION

SHARAM: Tom and Kate had a sitting with me. Kate is really afraid of sharing anything about her life with anyone. During their sitting, she had something she wanted to talk about, but she didn't want to do so in front of Tom because she thought he would use it against her later. So I asked Tom to leave. Afterwards, Kate started opening up and a lot of understanding came to her. I told her that the purpose of Tom being here was so that she could totally close her heart. Then, when she opened it, it became totally open. Totality. Totally you close, then when you open, that too will be total. Like the poles of a pendulum, the higher the pendulum swings in one direction, the higher it will swing in the opposite direction. When her heart opened, all this beautiful stuff came out in the sitting.

SHAHED: I was wondering why, when your heart is totally closed, does it go totally open, like in this case when Tom left?

SHARAM: Any totality makes you jump to transformation. Transformation in itself is total. So how can you jump to transformation? One way is for your heart to be totally closed. Then, all of a sudden your heart opens up totally, and you do the jump. Your soul will wake up and tell you what you need to know in that moment. Only what you need to know in that moment. That is all.

BALANCE

KATE: Everyone else is better than me. They have more politics. They know how to handle people, but I can't. Everybody hates me. Other people, like Roxana, are so right on. They know how to deal with people, but I can't.

SHARAM: Yes, you can. You do have subtlety when it is necessary, and you are hard and tough when it is necessary. You have that balance in the higher chakras. The balance is in dealing with people. Sometimes you are really strong and you hit people, not with your hand, but with the reality you feel at the time. Some people like Roxana always are political. If they have a problem with someone, they don't tell them. They just use politics to ease the situation. They don't get angry at people, but you get angry at times and are sweet at times. Some people don't have that balance, but you do. If you are always tough you are Hitler. If you are always sneaky about it, you become a politician. But if you have hardness and softness together, where does that balance come from? From the higher chakras.

THE POSITIVE WAY

KATE: When you tell me I have a problem, I hate it. I compare myself with others, and I hate myself.

SHARAM: There are two ways of looking at life. If you look at it positively, you will say, "Sharam, you are right. I do have this problem and I want to change it." The second way is the negative way. "I just found out that underneath what you are saying is I have a problem, and I hate this."

KATE: I feel like I have nothing to wake up for in the morning. Everything is a mess. I don't want to do anything anymore.

SHARAM: You don't want to wake up because you look at life in a negative way. When we look at life in a negative way, eventually we come down to feeling that there is nothing to live for. When you look at the positive, you look forward to going to transformation.

Let's look at how this works.

Over countless lifetimes, we have become used to the negative. Whenever there is something negative or we are negative, automatically, our psyche pushes it into the subconscious. But when we are positive, automatically, things come out of the subconscious. They come to the surface where we can look at them, work with them, and cleanse them. If we stay negative and allow negative thoughts to pile up over time, eventually they turn to "I don't have anything to live for."

On the contrary, if you look at things in a positive way, every morning, you will be really happy. There is so much positivity to look forward to, so many things to change. For example, "Today, I will share everything with everyone. Today I will be more courageous," versus getting up and saying, "I really don't want to get up. I have no purpose. I feel so awful."

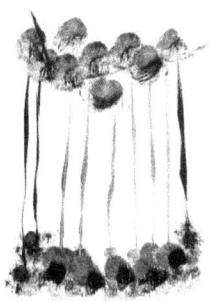

SINGING IN THE SHOWER

SHARAM: We sing in the shower because showering cleanses the karma and our hearts open; then we sing. In a sense, it is stepping outside the ego. When we cleanse the karma, we are not worried about anything and not worrying leads to singing out of joy. If we have heaviness on our mind, this singing does not happen.

MAKING A CONSCIOUS CHOICE

ANN: It feels impossible *(dropping the ego)*.

SHARAM: I said that we have to do something deliberately. What do I mean? I mean we must see it *(ourselves and our issues)*. There are good ways to not see it. One way is to think that you can't do anything, and then fall into your emotional body. I've noticed that every single time, when you fall into your emotional body, what you are really saying is "I don't want to do it right now, I don't want to look at myself right now." Another way is to be over-confident: "That's nothing, I can do it later." If you go to either of these two extremes, it means you are consciously deciding not to look at yourself. Right now you are consciously deciding not to see it. That's why you fall into "I can't do it. It's too much." Literally, you decide not to do it. I respect your decision, but at least know what you are doing. With having a teacher, you should know that much.

When I decide that I will do it, or when we say, "I just want to look at it, now," then *it* is done. This issue is totally broken. You might again go back to it, because the mind can't believe that you have changed. It takes a while for the mind to catch up, but eventually this issue becomes weak and goes away.

If you decide to be a watcher, then you are a winner.

> *"If we don't protect ourselves in the moment,
> we open a space in our conscious mind
> for the subconscious to pour into,
> and we have enough energy to actually
> look at what is coming out."*
>
> —Sharam

GENTLE CONTROLLING

SHAHED: I am feeling frustrated around this book, and how to proceed. I worry that I might become controlling.

SHARAM: You say you feel that you might become controlling. Control to a certain extent is wonderful. Without control you can't do anything. The right balance of control is vital, is necessary, and you have the softness now that combines with the controlling and makes it really juicy. You are afraid to do this book because you feel that your controlling may come out. Your controlling is really good now because it comes with the softness. So controlling is good as long as we bring the gentleness of the heart to it—controlling with the third and the fourth chakra combined.

Anything you want to do needs some part of the third chakra. But when it becomes too much, it becomes scary. Everybody is afraid of someone who has a very strong third chakra, even if the other is someone who is on the fifth or sixth chakra. Every chakra is afraid or has a little bit of fear of someone in the third chakra.

So you do have controlling, but your softness of the heart has been mixed together with it, so don't be afraid of it.

DROP THE SUGAR COATING!

LIVIA: I don't feel centered lately. I can't seem to get there. I feel aggressive, angry and not nice. I am everywhere and nowhere, which makes me anxiety-filled. I feel heavy, I get very abrasive.... I feel like the Livia that came here five years ago. For a long time you pleased my ego, which gave me a boost and I felt loved; I felt better about myself.

SHARAM: First, it was not pleasing your ego. It was genuine love, but your ego took it as "ego-boosting" because you don't know what genuine love is. Your ego took it as, "Look how great I am. Wow!"

LIVIA: Well something happened that I felt better about myself. I started to accept myself more, but that is not here now. I feel dissatisfied a lot of times. It seems that the only times I come to my heart are when I am here with you. What does that mean? Does that mean that the real me—you know the abrasive, pushing, controlling personality—is finally coming up?

SHARAM: Absolutely.

LIVIA: Well then, at least I feel that I am on track. It's so bad, I feel bad even sitting next to Roxana right now. I worry that she has to get all that negative energy from me and it makes me feel sad.

SHARAM: Roxana loves you very much and because she loves you very much, she doesn't get that energy. If she had any kind of resistance, however, she would get that energy.

LIVIA: Is there anything I could be doing more? I am so anxiety-filled, my heart is racing....

SHARAM: We could look at the reason for your anxiety, but the most important thing here is that you see your negativity, you see your abrasiveness. You have gotten rid of a lot of it, but *(miming wringing and squeezing stuff out of a bag.)* still we are pushing more and more of the negativity out.

LIVIA: When it comes up and out, like when I am abrupt or aggressive to others, I don't even feel bad and that makes me feel bad.

SHARAM: This is you—the real you is coming out. You didn't look at it before. Now you are looking at your ugliness. Thanks God that you are looking at your ugliness. Thank you. All this time you thought you were a nice lady by mistake....

LIVIA: ... very nice, as a matter of fact. *(Lots of laughter)*

SHARAM: Of course you are a nice lady when you are with your friends or your teacher, or you wouldn't have any friends, but I am glad you are seeing that. It is wonderful that you are seeing it, so wonderful. Remember, it's great that you see it. It is so nice to see that you see that you are not nice.

LIVIA: It is great, but, of course, my ego doesn't like to see or hear that I am ugly.

SHARAM: Of course! First of all your ego will say, "There is nothing wrong with me. I am nice!" But when you see something negative in yourself, you say, "It's horrible. My God, it's just terrible." Immediately, the ego looks for someone to blame. Anyone. "These meditations are no good. This Sharam is not good. My friends are no good. Never me. It's somebody else's fault." Or if it doesn't find anyone else at fault, then the heart pounds, anxiety comes, because it can't find anyone to blame.

This is really great that you know that the junk is coming out. You are honest and you are real—you are not sugar coating anymore. Thank you for saying this to me. It makes me feel so good. Thank you.

THROW THE ANGER OUT

CHRIS: I'm doing lots of exercises, but unlike others, I'm getting really angry. Why?

SHARAM: This is the anger that you were repressing before. It's becoming clearer and more expressive. In the past, years and years ago, you were collecting and holding in the anger. Today, as you go along and really are growing, the anger is coming more to the surface and out. It is a lot. It has always been a lot, but you were not advanced enough to express it. You were piling it up.

CHRIS: I feel I'm taking it out on other people.

SHARAM: That's usually what happens. Everyone goes through that. It is very natural. The good thing is that you can stop it soon. Maybe only a few months more that you will throw it on people. There are millions of people that are angry at other people all the time. For thirty, sixty, eighty years, maybe all their lives, they are angry people. You were behind almost everyone here *(at the ashram)* and outside. The advantage that you have over the outside world is that, with me, you have started to get the anger out. Within a short time we can manage it, and it will be gone. You won't have to throw it on other people. You are very lucky.

Let's recap. Especially in the West, people are angry. Let's say eighty-five percent of people in the West are angry. This is more advanced because the anger comes out. They throw it on other people and the anger comes out. You were behind, which means you were collecting it inside. You couldn't get angry at other people. You were hurting yourself. You were shoving it into your subconscious, into the basement of your soul. You were piling up and piling up a lot of anger.

Now, you really are dedicated. You really want to work on yourself. Today, thanks to your work, your meditations, your exercises, and your perseverance, the anger is really coming out. It's very natural to throw it on other people. But because you started with a teacher prior to becoming angry, when you become angry it is more manageable. You don't need to be in anger for years and years. In a sense, your soul held on to the anger waiting for me to come. When I came, gradually you brought it out. Now it is on the surface.

ASSERTIVENESS GIVES ME JUICE!

SHARAM: If I see assertiveness in any of you, it gives me juice. Even if I am tired, assertiveness wakes me up.

When you are strong and excited, not nagging or aggressive or passive, you will get anything you want. I promise you. This is the Law of Existence. Existence has promised that you will get what you want, if you know how to go about it.

If you are passive/aggressive, when you become aggressive things get done, but you get angry. You have to learn assertiveness. I am here to teach you how to go about being strong and decisive and assertive. If you, Chris, learn this, you graduate from Sharam's Mystical School. *(lots of laughter)* But, it is not the same for everyone. One student's core issue is different from another's.

Also, when you get frustrated, people don't hear you because people don't want to hear others' frustration. That is why you are not effective. You wait until you get frustrated before saying something. Then people respond by defending themselves. At that point, nothing gets done.

Being passive, on the other hand, is being harmful to yourself. It is aggression against the self. Aggression means aggression against others. So, you are either aggressive to yourself or aggressive to others and in a very subtle way, you are controlling. It is a combination of all the negativities of the lower chakras which creates the passive/aggressive.

ACCEPTANCE IS EVERYTHING

SHARAM: Basically, misery means nonacceptance. If you accept, there is no misery. If you accept ten percent, then you have ninety percent nonacceptance, so you have a lot of misery. Not total misery, but a lot. If you have fifty percent nonacceptance, then, fifty percent of you is miserable and the other fifty percent will be happy. The two will balance each other. You will feel hardship, but you will feel happiness too, so in general you will feel normal. If you accept ninety percent and ten percent you don't accept, you are basically a happy camper. You will be very close to ecstasy, because you are close to totality. If you accept, totally, there is no way you will be miserable. Acceptance is everything.

A year ago, we said that comparison is very harmful. Today we say, if there is no comparison, the mind basically cannot judge. Comparison brings judgment. When you say, this is beautiful, she is nice, this food is bad, or he is ugly…, how can you say someone is ugly? You compare with someone who is beautiful. If there is no comparison in the mind, all the judgments go away and you become content, totally.

HEART STRINGS

Did you know that your heart strings
Are attached to the corners of your mouth?
It's true!
And when you smile
It tugs them.
Try it! Right now!
Can you feel them?
Pulling your heart up?
Your happiness up?
Ahhh
Feels so good.
Let's do it again.

NEGATIVITY IS TOTALLY OPTIONAL

ANN: What about the fact that I choose negativity?

SHARAM: Negativity is totally optional. We absolutely have investments in negativity. Many times with negativity we get attention. Transformation gets instant attention. Negativity will also get instant attention; but with positivity, it depends. Sometimes when you are positive and someone else is negative, they get the attention because it is more of an emergency. When you are positive, others think you are fine, so they attend to the person who is negative. So positivity sometimes doesn't pay, whereas negativity pays all the time. People want to calm you down, attend to you, fix you, so they can be at peace and ease. They don't think they can be happy until you are better. Therefore, we have a great investment in negativity. Positivity will be good if other people are positive too, because then you get equal attention, but as soon as someone is negative, positivity looks blah. Now you know that the reason we stick to negativity is because it beats positivity for getting attention.

ANN: As long as you have ego, you need this attention?

SHARAM: The ego needs attention because the ego gets glorified with attention. The ego wants to be the most important. Attention serves that purpose—it makes us feel that we are more important. Why does ego want to be important? As a child, we were the center of the whole world. When we cried, we got attention. When we laughed, we got attention. People tickled us, played peek-a-boo with us. As a child, if you didn't get attention, you felt sad. Also, attention actually gives us more energy. When someone gives us attention, they give their kundalini energy to us and as children we learned that we needed that kundalini energy.

So when we grow up, we always want to be appreciated, we want attention, we want others to like us, because from childhood we associate attention with the extra energy it gave us. The ego enjoyed that extra soft energy we got from others. Now as adults, we want the enjoyment that loving energy gave us. If people ignore you, you don't get that joy, so we all learned some tricks from childhood to get attention. If you don't get it when you are happy, then you choose negativity and, for example, throw a temper tantrum. If someone here throws a temper tantrum, others feel left out. They get upset and decide, consciously or unconsciously, to throw tantrums too.

ANN: And just being more aware of this will help this?

SHARAM: Sure. When you are more aware, you will see the tricks of this whole business and how you are negative and how you are miserable. Gradually you become sick and tired of it.

ANN: Being positive will be enough at that point?

SHARAM: No. Then you want to go to transformation. With the transformative you will be in ecstasy. You open the door to Existence and you get juice from everywhere. You won't need the attention of others. If you are in transformation, you get energy from everyone. If you are in transformation, beyond good and bad, positivity and negativity, you feel the juice of all Existence. If you are not enlightened you close the door to all this energy. Enlightenment, or transformation, means having the door open. Then you get the juice from all of Existence, even that pigeon flying out there. That pigeon is giving you juice. You only get it when you are enlightened, otherwise you have closed the door. You don't get the juice.

ANN: So until we are enlightened, we don't feel the transformative? Or do we have moments?

SHARAM: We get moments.

ANN: How do we get past the negative while we still are not enlightened?

SHARAM: By observation, watchfulness.

WORRYING MEANS "I AM IMPORTANT"

Commenting on negativity being a choice and that watching it is the answer to switching negativity to positivity, Shahed gave the example of going to the DMV and getting stressed out about how to get in and out of there the quickest, given the crowds and long waits.

SHAHED: We got there before they opened and I watched myself, as more people showed up, stressing out about forming a line. I didn't want anyone to cut in front of me. I was aware that I was creating stress for myself, that I was acting crazy, but that awareness or watching did nothing to help me transform it to positivity or relaxation. How could I have transformed all that rush and stress into relaxation?

SHARAM: How do we change that negativity, that anxiety, to positivity and hopefully to transformation? I said that we create the negativity. It is optional. We do it. There is a deep fear in us that if we don't worry about something, like this line at the DMV, for instance, we might not have anything else to do. There is a deep fear that we might get bored. The ego wants to be important and if we worry about these things, really, to ourselves and to others, we look important. It's that simple, wanting to show, to ourselves at least, that we are important. Worrying about something in the language of ego means, "I am important."

They told us from childhood, "You need to be careful. You need to pay attention." It's really like they are telling us, "You need to worry. If you are careless, it's bad." I don't want to say that they told us to worry, but indirectly they did. "Get your education. Get good grades. You have to pay your dues. You have to do it." Almost they are telling us to be worried over and over. If you are not worried about it, that's bad. So they are telling us, "Don't relax." This is how we learn to worry about things, to care too much. So this is the ego. Ego believes that if you don't worry, you are not important.

SHAHED: I do this in two ways. Like with the DMV, for example, I know that I can do the DMV. I have the confidence that I can make my way through it, but I am still hypervigilant, and want to do it in the best way possible so I don't waste time and am not taken advantage of by others. But I also do it in another way. I overworry so that I can't move forward with a project. I freeze or procrastinate forever. This type of worrying seems counterproductive to the ego's goal of feeling important.

SHARAM: Yes, negativity is counterproductive. You want to be productive for only one reason, so people will like you. This whole thing about worrying is that, "If I worry, I am a good person and people will like me, so I get the attention." You want to be productive so people like you, and you worry so people will like you, but because worrying is counterproductive, they're not going to like you anyway. But I want you to know that here I don't care about productivity. We can work on that book for the rest of our lives, or we can drop it and everything is great. We are here to look at our worrying. The funny thing is that when we look at our worrying and notice how it is attached to the ego, and that the ego wants to be liked, gradually, when the worry comes, you say "Ahh ha! I know this. This is the ego and the ego wants to be liked, and I'm doing all this just to be liked?" We start to see how crazy worrying is. And when we see that, all of a sudden, you are productive for the right reason, just to be productive, not to be liked.

Every time that we want to be liked, it will lead to worrying. Just be sensitive and say to yourself, "Look, now I am worried that these people have to be in a line, but why do they have to be in a line? I get my job done and I am out of here. They can be as offline as they want to. *(lots of laughter)* I still will get my job done; I still will get out of here and they still won't be in a line and they don't have to if they don't want to."

SHARAM REVIEWING: When you worry, remember it is about wanting to be liked. We have been trained wrongly that we need to be concerned, so concerned that our concern has changed to worry. They told us, "You need to be concerned. You need to do well, or be good in this." Being too concerned has pushed us over the edge. It is just too much pressure. Here we learn that you need to be good, but also you need to be bad. You need to be transformed, but if you think you need to be transformed, you never become transformed because you think you need to. There is no need. You are just perfect as you are. You are God. It is so perfect to be you. Also it is so perfect to be me. Don't be me. Let me be me. You be you.

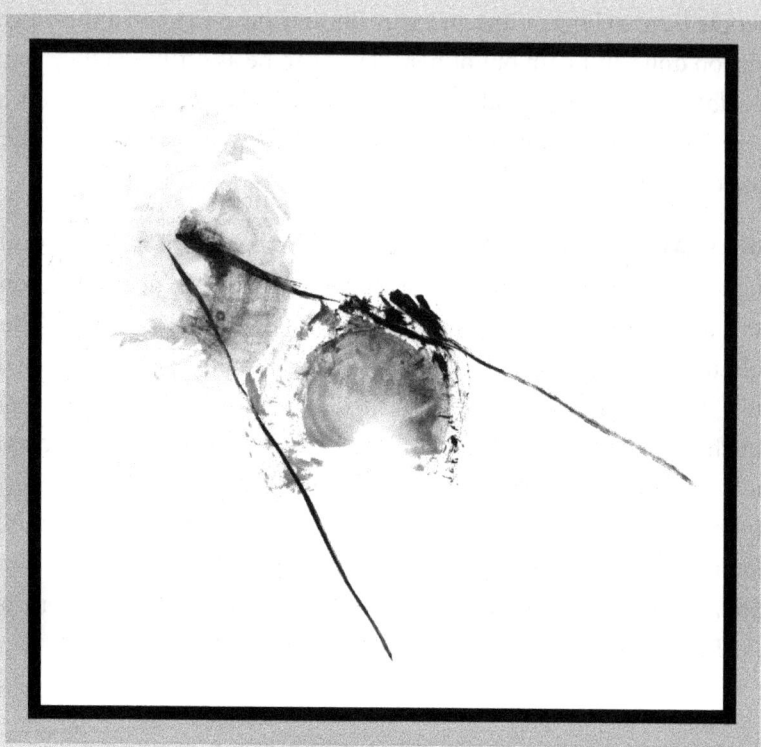

BAD AND GOOD

Sharam had asked Rabia to write one thousand times, "There is no good and no bad." After that, he asked her to use a rosary and say to herself one thousand times a day, "There is no good and no bad," for one month. Then, Rabia did something that Sharam said was bad.

RABIA: How does bad exist, if there is no bad and there is no good?

SHARAM: We do not exist, so we don't do things. Only God exists, so only God is doing. So something God did was bad, but all bad is necessary.

Bad is the root of the tree, good is the branches of the tree. The fruit is the transformation. We don't eat the roots or the branches, we eat the fruit, but without the roots and the branches, we won't have any fruit. So without good and bad, we won't have any transformation.

Right now, we live for bad and good, but that is not living. The sooner we find out that those are not the main thing, that the main thing is to eat the fruit, the better. You can have a huge tree with strong roots, but without the fruit, you will still be hungry. You will be so miserable, so spiritually dead. There is no transformation, no going above good and bad. You might die of hunger but the tree is still there. Now we see the fruit, the transformation, is the point.

So what is negativity? It is there for us to understand positivity. What is positivity? Positivity is there for us to understand negativity. They both exist so we can go above and beyond them. Negativity makes you feel yucky. Positivity makes you feel good. With transformation you go beyond feeling yucky, beyond happiness and beyond having fun. Transformation is ecstasy, happiness and fun multiplied by a billion.

RABIA: Is the only way to get to transformation, to go through good and bad?

SHARAM: The only way to get to transformation is one thing and one thing only—for you to understand that God is creating every single moment. Every single moment, Existence is happening, but we come in and we want to improve on Existence. We want to do something better. We want to change something. We don't like something.

We've been told, something is good, something has value and something else is junk. Then we always want to get the valuable. We have to do something that is worthwhile. Right now, we are not good enough. You've got to do something good. In this way, you spoil your moment. We think we need to do this or that, or that we are behind on some project, for example, and we should be working on it rather than what is happening now. You want to improve on God and that is suffering just because of good and bad.

This moment is so perfect. What does it mean that I'm behind or I didn't get my job done, or I'm worried about this moment? This moment is so perfect and the next moment is like this moment. All we have to do is not push and pull so much.

"I am Existence pretending that I'm Rabia."

–*Sharam*

CONNECTION WITH EXISTENCE

ANN: I really have a need to connect with you. Why?

SHARAM: When you connect with me, deep inside you know I don't have an ego, so at least half of the work is done. You don't need to work to get the ego of the other person to step aside. We only need to work with *your* ego and even that is mostly my job—to bring you to the brink of making the jump from ego to no ego.

FINDING YOUR CENTER

LEILA: Why do I lose my center?

SHARAM: Because the center that you have is limited. You don't have a full center. You have a tiny bit of center, and you can lose that tiny bit of center with the smallest disagreements, smallest negativity. If you had a complete center, if you were not there yourself and Existence was, then you would never lose that. You still have ego as the center, and ego always falls apart.

LEILA: How can I gain a center?

SHARAM: With a deeper understanding of how stupid good and bad are, and that in reality there is no good and bad. Understanding this breaks a big conditioning for us because most of our conditionings are related to good and bad. You want to be a good girl and you are teaching your daughter to be one too. I am not saying not to teach her. She needs to think that good and bad exist. But you have to break that conditioning *(for yourself)*. If you understand this deeply, you will find a real center in your life.

You put your center on something that you have learned from society, which is false. When this conditioning falls apart, you lose your center and wonder why. It is because your center is based on a false notion, a false understanding, a false concept, a conditioning. But if you build your center on the right understanding, on the Laws of Existence, then you will never fall apart.

The Laws of Existence always apply, and one Law of Existence says that everything about our lives starts from within, starts with us. Others are neutral. You determine what happens around you and who does what, whether you are conscious of this or not. When you know this, then you won't blame others and you won't need to fall apart.

THE BITCH

This sitting had to do with fully accepting what is happening for you in the moment. For example, Livia said she has been a real bitch lately and Sharam said, "Not just lately, but forever." He then told Livia to just be a bitch for awhile. Stop trying to be nice and just be the bitch. If your energies inside are not fighting each other, then this energy moves so easily everywhere. You are not dissipating energy. The energy is not getting lost in fighting with yourself. Then that energy, that extra energy, can be used for anything: for happiness, for healing, for your growth, awareness, whatever.

THE BITCH

Let the bitch out of the closet,
Let that bitch sing
Stop pasting on a smile
That makes your face sting.

We all know that she's in there
You're not hiding a thing
So let the bitch out of the closet
So we can send her packing.

ON EXPRESSING

SHARAM: Someone asked me, "If I express, will that take care of everything and will all the negativity go away?" I said, yes. The only reason we are negative is because we can't express.

ANN: But the other day, because I expressed myself and another student thought I was acting superior, I fell into negativity, and I'm still there.

SHARAM: You expressed and then you went to negativity and you stayed there. Existence wants you to stay in it, to go deeper. Then, when you come up, you bring a big chunk of karma up too and with transformation, it gets thrown out. So Existence wants you to cleanse. That's why it doesn't quickly bring you out, because it wants you to stay in negativity to go deeper, to cleanse not only this new karma, but to cleanse a chunk of old, deeper karma too.

You should express, sound superior, and then look at it and learn from it. Express more and sound superior and look at your feeling superior. If you go to inferiority, that too is ego. Watch it. If you watch and grab a hold of your ego, then all of a sudden prana *(energy)* comes around you. You get refreshed. Existence rejoices! Everyone rejoices!

ANN: I can't accept those things in me I see are bad.

SHARAM: You don't need to accept it if you can't. If you *can* accept it, accept it, but, if you cannot, let's open it. When we open things, you accept. If I tell you to accept and you say you can't accept, I can't force you to accept. I'm saying *don't* accept, but let's talk about it. Let's open it up. All of a sudden we reach to acceptance together.

ANN: I listen to recordings of my sittings. On them, all I do is ask how to change what I am. I don't accept *anything*. I don't see any way out.

SHARAM: There is no way out. You are *in*. We have to work from within. You don't need to come out of it. You are in this "not accepting." It's wrong if I keep telling you to accept. I'm not going to say that anymore. I'm going to say, it's okay *not* to accept. *(Ann starts to smile, to soften.)* You see right there you are accepting that it's okay not to accept.

Let's just open the issue. Let's look at it. When you understand, the acceptance comes with that understanding. You don't need to accept.

You shared something you knew. I liked it. I didn't think you were superior or inferior. I don't think sharing something you know is superiority. I was there. You weren't being superior. If Rabia said she felt that you were, that is something that Rabia has to go through; it is something she needs to resolve in herself. You were not trying to be superior. Trust me.

This is why we are here. My teaching is useless if we don't apply it, if we don't look at ourselves. If someone gets offended, let them talk. Let's open the issue. Let's see what Rabia's problem is.

Everyone is here to open themselves, to understand, to learn, to grow. Nothing else. I don't want you to sit here and behave. It's not about behaving. It's about deeper understanding and opening everything that you feel. It's not about behaving or getting something done. It's about the moment and exploring the moment. Let's say I have something planned for a class, but we open an issue instead. The spur of the moment, what happens in the moment, is the best. If you share something, it is really good. Your openings are really helping many people.

ANN: I withdraw for so many days and am afraid to say anything to anyone. Where does that come from?

SHARAM: It comes from the issue with your mother. You are afraid to open that issue. It comes from the past lifetime. It comes from within you.

ANN: So I still haven't opened that issue after all this time?

SHARAM: This is the deepest issue, Ann. "After all that time?" If this is resolved, you will be enlightened. So we keep chipping away at it. We keep digging things up and throwing them out. This is real. Trust me. Believe me, Ann. If this is resolved, totally, you will be enlightened. Don't ever say, "After all this time, I haven't resolved this yet." This is a deep, deep, deep, deep thing. Actually, you're so simple. This problem with your mother is the only problem you have. Really.

This is the one issue you have, and we are working on it. When you finish this one thing, then you are with God. That's a big order. Give some time to it. You waited many lifetimes for this. A few years more is nothing.

ANN: It seems like it keeps getting worse. It's not getting better.

SHARAM: Every time you go to the negative, to that one problem, you go deeper, and it looks worse. Of course it looks worse, because you go deeper in the negativity. You keep cleaning and go deeper. On the surface it seems not bad. As you go deeper, it is more compressed, so it is worse. If you say, "As I go deeper it's getting better," then I know you are not getting it.

(To the group) When an issue looks worse, what does it really mean? That it is getting better because we are going deeper into this pocket of negativity and throwing it out. You are getting closer to the end of the tunnel where the light is—the light at the end of the tunnel—you are getting closer to it. All this condensed stuff from way back is coming out.

AN ANGEL IN WHITE

Be free my love
For words
Are your freedom
Let them flow
For your own joy

Unlock the rabid beast
Angered only by the congestion
Of words and letters
Encircling him like a cell.
Release him and you will see
As letters clear,
An angel in white
Emerging here.

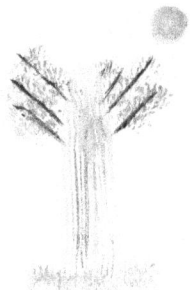

INFERIORITY LEADS TO SUPERIORITY

ANN: For me one of the worst sins I could commit is to be superior. I was wondering if I should open it up.

SHARAM: We want to use everything we can, watching, understanding, meditating over it, focusing totally on it. Watching and focusing are two different things. When I say focus on it, I mean almost deliberately creating it. Your whole life should be focused on this. When I say watch it, I mean every time it comes up, look at it. When I say meditate on it, I mean to think about it. Understanding means to keep opening it up with me. Think about it. Write it down, even essays on superiority. We have to attack it from every angle. Don't just watch it. Do everything.

ANN: So can you help me with understanding?

SHARAM: If you want understanding, every time we have a sitting, you should be right here talking about it, so it goes deeper all the time.

Superiority. If you have that, it means you do have inferiority. What does inferior mean? It means less than. Not important enough. Not good enough. If you think like that, then you try to show the opposite; you try to act superior. Do you have an inferiority complex? Do you think you are not good enough?

ANN: You have said many times, I don't feel deserving. Is feeling inferior the same as not feeling deserving? Is that one of the reasons I am so negative here? Because I am afraid to go to the positivity, because when I go to the positivity, that superiority comes out?

SHARAM: Yes, you do have that fear. We've learned from today that if you have an inferiority complex, you will act like you are superior, and you will feel like you don't deserve. For example, you don't feel you deserve coming back and knocking at my door, and you have problems with thinking people don't want to be with you. The acting superior also comes from this. You want to hide feeling inferior. Ego comes from it.

ANN: Also, I have been totally exhausted. I just want to sleep. Is this a side effect of what is going on?

SHARAM: Exactly. Just know that when there is a war, U.S./Iraq war, so many resources go to this war, almost to the verge of the economy breaking down. Inner war is the same thing. If you are fighting with yourself, two opposite things are fighting, superior/inferior, then you get exhausted all the time because energy gets wasted. War is a very costly thing. Inner war is exactly like the outer war.

ANN: Is the reason it is exhausting me is because I don't accept?

SHARAM: War basically means not accepting. Two forces are not accepting. If one force accepts, the other will do the same. The war stops. Of course it is not accepting.

TAKING RESPONSIBILITY

SHARAM: You get involved in other people's issues. That's the problem. If, instead of wanting to look at someone else's ego, or their issues, you look at yourself, Existence sends you fresh prana energy which will be really a blessing. It makes you so soft, all of a sudden, miracles happen for you. But if you constantly want to look at someone else's faults, you create a heavy negative energy around you that takes you to a closed heart, and you get disturbed…, unhappy. For example, why did Rabia do that or Sophie do that?

ANN: I thought more that I was worrying about how I was affecting them.

SHARAM: That is also a problem. When you worry about how you are affecting others, you are indirectly criticizing them. Did you know that? It is very subtle, but it is true. You are saying they are not mature enough to handle you. They are a kid. If they were an adult, they could handle this. Instead of asking them if you have bothered them, you are assuming. That is criticizing. If they say they have an issue with you, if you want to withdraw, escape, again you are criticizing them. You are putting them down. If they have an issue with you, try to stay centered, work with them to resolve that issue, instead of protecting yourself.

Any time you assume, or want to escape, or carry these issues around in your mind for long periods without resolving them ... all that is criticizing, putting people down, making hardships for people. If someone has a problem with you, if you really are concerned for others, you will say "I really want to solve this. I don't want to cause problems for you. I really want to work on this." But what do you do? You protect yourself. You yell at them, saying "Well then it is your own fault." Or you say "Then I had better get out of here". These are all punishments for others.

ANN: I know. I'm horrible. This is all that this is coming down to. I don't know what to do about it. Opening it up does nothing but expose how bad I am. And now, I'll just go sit outside for three days and think about how bad I am.

SHARAM: You say it in a way that you want to say it is someone else's fault. You are not taking responsibility. When you throw a temper tantrum, you don't take responsibility. You just want to make someone else feel guilty. You want to make other people responsible, like a child that throws temper tantrums. What you are really saying is that you want something from me. I'm supposed to go out there and bring you in. That is what you are telling me.

ANN: No. This is what I do. I go out there for days. This is what I have been doing. It's not your fault or my fault. It is just what I am doing.

SHARAM: It's not your fault?

ANN: *(Angry)* Okay it is. Everything is my fault. That is the point.

SHARAM: When you throw a temper tantrum by saying, "*Everything* is my fault," you are basically saying "*Nothing* is my fault. It is *your* fault." It is a very subtle thing. You don't see it. You don't want to see it. You think it is my fault, or those people standing in the hallway. It is their fault. You really don't want to take responsibility. That is the problem.

ANN: So what should I do?

SHARAM: Take responsibility. Taking responsibility is an active way to break something that doesn't make sense. Taking responsibility means to change.

ANN: But, I can't change.

SHARAM: The only reason you can't change is because you don't want to take responsibility. In a very subtle way, you want to make everyone feel guilty. It is their fault. That is the only reason you don't change. Believe me. Scratch the surface a little bit, and a little bit deeper in you is, "It is Sharam's fault. I can't connect with him. Everyone else gets to, but I don't. He is not here. He is asleep." Even if you *(Ann)* are at work, it is my fault that we are not connecting. Everything is everybody else's fault. You don't say it because it doesn't make sense, but that is exactly what is there. It is everybody else's fault. As soon as you really see that it is you, then you say, "Again it is all my fault. I'm horrible." What you are really saying is, "Of course it is not my fault. It is their fault." You don't verbalize it, but that is what you are saying. Watch what you are saying. If you truly, truly see that it is your doing, you would change it, but you don't want to. You want to say that it is everybody else's fault. Believe me. Do you see what I am saying?

ANN: I'm not getting it.

SHARAM: Maybe it is not about getting. You will listen to the tape many times. This is the best thing that ever happened for Ann, today. The very best. All the truth, Existence brought out for you. *(Ann begins to cry.)* Come closer and give me a hug. *(Giving Ann a hug while she cries herself out)* I've never seen so much clarity in connecting with you. I just love you. All these things we talk about are your inner work, but I love you just the way you are. Even the little child in you that throws temper tantrums I really love. If I talk to you like this, it is because you want to grow up, you want to see yourself. Personally, I don't care if you change because I love you just the way you are, but for your sake, if you grow, you will be happier.

Sharam is very firm with the ego, but always loving of the being, the soul. Watching a sitting like this, where the student's ego continually resists is very difficult, but at the same time it is very touching. As students, we begin to see that, no matter how badly we fall into the trap of our ego, Sharam will still love us. It goes a long way in garnering courage to continue to battle our egos, and more importantly to expose them to the group and Sharam, when we know we have this kind of support.

INTO LOVE AGAIN

*My mind is strong and knowing
That of love, there's no such thing,
But soul, tethered to mind's dark walls
Forgets as, again, love takes wing.*

*But soon comes mind, sabotaging
As tether gets drawn tight
Watching with grief and longing
As beloved continues on with flight.*

*But then came you ...
And though mind writhed and twisted,
The patient wings of love persisted.*

*Tirelessly you've stayed with me
As I retreat to mind's dark walls
A light in devil's doorway
Renewing Love's call.*

*Years later, tether's frayed
Ankle bleeding and calloused
But as we fly together at rope's end
Joy weakens minds malice*

*I know you will not leave me,
No matter how I kick and scream,
And one day, rotten rope will snap
And we'll fly away on Ecstatic breeze.*

PASSIVITY COMES FROM FEAR

STREAM: Ann' sitting was very useful for me. I came here wondering whether I should open up about something that was bothering me. But my mind was finding reasons to put it off, which is something that I always do. Then you invited Ann to come up for a sitting. Meanwhile, I'm still going on in my head about my issue, watching the time…, thinking, "Why did Sharam ask Ann up? Why are they going on so long?" So here I am throwing the responsibility from me onto both of you.

SHARAM: Wow! Thank you. Big lesson for you. This is something … I've been trying to bring out in you for so many years, and you did it just now. I hope it's a real breakthrough for you. You chuck your growth for conditionings like, "A lady has to be graceful" or "I shouldn't be aggressive." Things like that. Really asking to be first in the sitting is assertive. It makes sense. You have to go *(to work)*. You know that the sitting might take a long time with anyone else. Everyone understands that you have to go. But I'm glad that you sat here through it, because, otherwise, you wouldn't have had this experience.

STREAM: I think many times I don't come up here because I still have a fear of looking bad in front of these beautiful people. It's not them. It's some kind of a fear that I retain from my upbringing.

SHARAM: No wonder how much I make you look bad in front of everyone, because of that fear! I often call you Cheap Charlie or this and that ... because of that fear.

STREAM: Yeah. So there's still a deep fear inside me.

SHARAM: Okay, so we look at your deep fear more often now. Let's go to your original question. The issue.

Stream speaks about her issue with Baba, another student, and then says...

STREAM: I'm trembling like crazy and I don't know why.

SHARAM: What is the reason? We have to find out.

STREAM: I think I'm just nervous about having said all of that. I love Baba so dearly. At the same time, I've said some really ugly stuff. Maybe that's what it is.

SHARAM: You can't be real? You have to always watch what you're saying? You can't be just absolutely real?

When you don't come and sit here *(in front of the group)*, when you are passive, that passivity comes from fear. But, today for a change you became assertive, and you're really afraid of it. You feel so safe in your passivity. You didn't know the reason you were trembling. That's fantastic. Do you guys see? She didn't know the reason. Why didn't you know the reason? Because this part is so hidden in you. You don't know about it. Today, maybe right now, is the first time you saw why you are so passive; so much fear that people might not like you. Fantastic!

"*All thinking is out of fear. The more fear…, the more you think. No fear, thinking stops.*"

"*Focusing on the body while breathing pulls fear to the surface, spreads it out, makes it thinner…. As the fear thins, the mind slows down and with a slower mind, love can happen.*"

–Sharam

ANXIETY IS GOOD

The next three sittings happened as one, but again, they are divided by subject matter.

Livia was talking to Sharam about projects at home and how they created anxiety around the deadline. The mess/paperwork/etc. of her home is always an issue for Livia and, because her brother and sister were coming to stay for a month, she felt more pressure to get the place cleaned up. Sharam has given her a deadline to get everything done before they get here.

LIVIA: I am very excited about the clean-up project of my garden, house, and paperwork before my siblings get here in September, but anxiety comes up that I won't finish on time. I don't like this anxiety. I don't sleep well, and it makes me crazy. I seem to be obsessed with the projects. There is this urgency behind it that makes me nervous. Can you help me with that?

SHARAM: Urgency is good and the anxiety is good, also. You get something done. Stay with the anxiety until your brother and sister come. There is no harm in it. It is okay to be on your toes for a while, to be anxious. The reason we don't like a disturbance—to be anxiety ridden—is because we don't want it to be there. It's there and we don't want it. When you don't want something, even if it is joy, it is going to harm you. But if you don't mind and accept, even something that is harsh is going to be joyful for you. Even horrible misery, if you accept it, becomes joyful. It's a matter of resisting versus accepting.

The anxiety comes because of the time frame; but you don't like anxiety, you think it's bad. That's where it hurts you. Anytime we don't want something, it is going to hurt us. But if you say anxiety is necessary—wow—then it becomes exciting. You see, if you have acceptance, even for anxiety, then anxiety will give you a lot of joy and energy. If you think it's bad, all your energy gets thrown out.

LIVIA: It makes sense to me because of a previous talk with you when you asked me to just be that bitch that I felt I was, but always tried to cover up with being nice. You asked me to welcome that bitch, to be happy it was there, to welcome it's presence and to let it have its way. "Just be bitchy and to hell with the people that don't like it. That's their problem." Ever since then I haven't been bitchy.

SHARAM: You've always been bitchy. *(Lots of laughter, Livia included)*

LIVIA: Well, all of last week I wasn't bitchy—ever since you "allowed" me to be that bitch.

SHARAM: Livia, the only time that you are not a bitch is when you have a transformation.

LIVIA: Even last week?

SHARAM: No, last week—that worked. You've always been a bitch. That is wonderful—that is you—and I like it. You accepted your bitchiness last week. I have accepted your bitchiness for years, and the group also.

Livia thanks Sharam and the group for their love and acceptance.

LIVIA: I loved what you said to Ann earlier, that you just love us the way we are and the reason why you talk a bit firm to us sometimes is only so that our lives could be a bit better.

SHARAM: That means that I accept you the way you are. My life is great with you guys. Your bitchiness is so wonderful to me. Because I accept you, you love me and you reciprocate that love. I gave you total space from the beginning, so you understood that this was a space for you where you could grow and that was safe. Because you are a bitch, you want quality. If there weren't any quality, you wouldn't go for that. When you accepted your bitchiness, you learned that whenever you accept something, that thing will step aside.

This is what I do—my secret to working with you guys. I walk into your life with accepting you totally, so your issues step aside. So, there is a big lesson here: **Acceptance causes any issue that we have accepted to step aside, whether it's in us or in somebody else.** Again a transformation happened to you.

WRONG IS RIGHT, RIGHT IS RIGHT

Livia described how she is also noticing how opinionated she is and that criticism stems from having opinions.

SHARAM: Being opinionated is helping you, as well as being a bitch, and there is nothing wrong with that. Why is it not wrong? Existence has given these things to you to help you. If Existence wouldn't have given you bitchiness, you would have gotten jealousy, for example, or poverty, or so much money that you would also have gotten all those sicknesses that come with having so much money. Existence has given you bitchiness and opinionatedness because that is helping *you*. So, whoever you are is a blessing. Everything is absolutely one hundred percent necessary, and there is nothing that is wrong. That's why we say there is no good or bad. If there is nothing wrong, everything is right, all the time, so right doesn't have any meaning anymore, because if everything is right, ***everything*** is great. When there is nothing bad then the word "bad" has no meaning. The word "bad" has given the meaning to the word "good;" "wrong" has given the meaning to "right," but if there is nothing wrong, there is nothing right either. Everything is as it is. And I can't even say "perfect" because then again there is nothing "imperfect."

DON'T BE GREEDY

Livia has been having problems with her hip. She opened the issue with Sharam who told her it was related to her first chakra. This sitting occurred at the end of the previous sitting regarding anxiety and acceptance. By the end of this sitting, Livia had been sitting in front of Sharam for a long time, thus his comment, "Don't be greedy."

SHARAM: It's related to being cheap. Don't think of it as being bad. As long as you stick to worrying about means and finances you will have that problem. You are holding onto a lot of karma in that area.

LIVIA: What can we do? It seems to be getting worse, not better.

SHARAM: Yes, it will really take you down. Let's take the example with your investment of forty thousand dollars, which is a lot of money to be stuck somewhere. *(Livia lost forty thousand dollars in a bad investment.)* Really, deep inside, you wanted to show yourself that you don't need that money. You don't need any money, but you don't listen to it. It is amazing how one issue *(pause)* I am so glad this is happening with your hip, because it gives you a sense of urgency that you have to do something about this. *(Sharam has been working on Livia's first chakra from the beginning. He has challenged her repeatedly to do things that* *would work directly on that karma. Often she resists.)* I am so glad that your spirit is high. You keep going forward, you try to fix it and you are not so worried about it, which is good. But there is this heaviness around the first chakra. Roxana can show you some exercises for that. Alright?

Besides bringing energy to this area, you have to resolve these money issues. Nobody can heal your chakras but yourself.

LIVIA: Can you give me more help?

SHARAM: Don't be greedy—not even right now. Start with these exercises and we'll take it from there. The ultimate exercise for you is:

DON'T BE GREEDY !!!

CRYING CLEANSES KARMA

DEBBY: My life in the outside world is working well, but I'm crying all the time. What is going on?

SHARAM: Crying is an act of expression involving both the second and fifth chakras. The crying happens when the energy moves from the second chakra *(emotional body)* to the fifth chakra *(expression center)*. This causes the tears. When you are going back and forth between these two chakras, a lot of emotional baggage gets thrown out. When the tears go on for a long time, it means there is totality in the throat and huge chunks of karma pour out. When you are with me, you get an extra boost of energy from my kundalini. You use this extra energy to move back and forth between these two chakras and lots of cleansing happens.

LOVE AND FREEDOM

MONA: Why do I have so much fear of losing those I love?

SHARAM: That is a very old wound that you have brought from a past lifetime. That's why you chose the family that you did, one in which whenever problems arise, someone always says, I'm going to leave.

MONA: Why do I always think that no one wants me?

SHARAM: You should know that nobody wants you, or anyone. The amount of love that you give is exactly the amount of love you get back. You determine the amount. You are the decision maker. People want others to love them; that's why you look for love, because you want people to want you.

So the power really lies in your hands. Nobody can leave you. In fact, nobody is free to leave you because everybody is so much conditioned, so much unconscious, that if somebody loves them, they want to stay with them. Love is almost taking their freedom away.

When somebody loves you, you feel so happy that you want to stay with that person. You don't have a choice. You are lacking love, somebody gives you that love, you really enjoy it, so you stay with them. You can go any time you want, but you *won't* go. You still feel free. You think you chose this, but love holds you. So in a sense you are not free. But love, plus working on yourself and having deeper understanding, gets you to love *and* freedom.

When you become enlightened, you have absolute freedom, you are totally free. Free of conditionings, free of unconsciousness. So what we do here by working on ourselves, we are moving closer and closer to that total freedom. We have to know that we are not free, and that we have to work towards becoming more and more free. It's very interesting. If somebody loves you, they take your freedom away. Love alone is not enough. Meditation, understanding, breathing exercises, and love will get you closer and closer to that absolute freedom.

TORRY: So unless you are enlightened, you can't have love and freedom? You can have love, but you don't have freedom?

SHARAM: Right. Enlightened means freedom. Before enlightenment you don't have freedom. You might feel love, but you don't have freedom. If I only loved you—if I didn't teach you breathing exercises, if we didn't have sittings, if there wasn't deeper more subtle understandings—I would be taking your freedom away. But if I love you *and* work with you towards freedom, I am giving you love, and in the near future, freedom.

SHARAM: *(To Mona)* You have reached a certain maturity now that you can understand this with all your being. To become mature means to know that nobody is in charge but you.

MONA: What is love?

SHARAM: The first thing is to give freedom to the other person, but first you have to make sure that you are capable of giving freedom to yourself. If you give freedom to yourself, then you can give it to others. Giving freedom to the self comes from self-confidence.

Compassion is also very important, but there should be a balance between compassion and strength. Together these two make a beautiful balance. For instance, you should have politics, which means using the mind in order to *not* hurt other peoples' egos, but you have to be firm and real. There should be a balance between politics and being real. And always you have to tell the truth. Using the mind to bring in constructive politics helps with this. Definitely you have to be real and tell the truth.

MONA: What is self-confidence?

SHARAM: Self-confidence means to put your focus on what are you capable of. Know that you are really working on yourself and that you have worth. Even if you do meditation for half an hour, make it real. Don't be wishy-washy about it. Whatever you know how to do, do it well. And be real. For example, the love I feel from you right now is very real.

LOVE AND FREEDOM CONTINUED

SHARAM: At the time of Buddha, every time someone became enlightened, Master would say, "You go and work with people. You don't stay with the master. You are a master yourself. You have to go to different towns and give what you have to others." When you are a disciple of the path and not enlightened yet, you always want to go out and work with people, but when you become enlightened, you don't have an ego anymore, so you go with what Existence tells you. You don't have a will of your own. Only God has will in you. You are a vehicle of God, of Existence.

"Freedom is not more important than love because freedom comes from inside of love. If love becomes an imprisonment, then freedom seems more important, but if the love moves to more and more freedom… then the love goes on forever and ever and ever."

–Sharam

EXISTENTIAL INTERFERENCE

MAHSA: Real happiness should come from within us. Right?

SHARAM: Real happiness does come from within us. It's not that it should come from, it does come. When we say "should" we are interfering. The only reason we are on Earth is to give space to Existence to happen without interference. It's only our interfering that makes us unhappy.

MAHSA: Why don't I have patience to finish something?

SHARAM: We learn from society and parents that when we start something, we've got to finish it, but really this is empty. It doesn't mean much. The people who are really smart, it's hard for them to finish something totally because it doesn't have challenge for them. It loses its importance. Many very smart people didn't finish school or, like Einstein, were poor students and struggled to finish.

"*God said,
'I am who I am,'
Not
'I am who I should be.'*"

–Sharam

THE DIAMOND IN THE ROUGH

FARIN: Harshness is a big problem for me. If anyone becomes harsh, I really get hurt. You told me I have this problem from my past lifetime and that I have to pass this stage and become okay with it *(harshness)*. But I think to be okay with harshness, you either have to be so gross or you should be enlightened. Then, harshness won't bother you.

SHARAM: Or you let yourself be bothered by harshness. If you are looking for grace, you have to learn the thirst. Instead of looking for water, learn how to be thirsty. If you are thirsty and you quickly drink, you don't learn how to be thirsty. So get hurt by harshness and know that no matter whether you are enlightened or gross, you will be bothered by it.

We should know that harshness exists, and you need to learn what to do with it. You have to learn to work with it and to pull the gentleness out of it. In any harshness, there is a gentleness. Find it, bring it out, focus on the gentleness in the harshness, the diamond in the rough.

In every harshness, there is a softness. You just need to find it. That is my job as a mystic. I look at students in front of me. They are harsh. I always look for that softness in the rough. When I convey it to them, they become very happy. They learn that even in the roughness is softness.

We don't see the softness in the harshness. We only see the harshness. Some people only look at the softness. They see the harshness but they know it's not very important. They have passed the negative state and have gone to the positive. When you are in the positive, you see both the positive and negative, but only the positive matters.

You see someone is lying and cheating. They don't fool you, but you focus on their smile, something positive. That positivity can grow and take over their whole being if you focus and work on their positive aspects.

I want to give the example of Roxana *(another student)*. These days she is doing lots of meditation and is working hard on herself. At the same time, I have been so harsh with her, but all the time she pulls the softness from it. She does it in a way that I could become embarrassed if I had an ego. This is how I work with her, by becoming very harsh. A year ago, just a little harshness from me would make her so hurt. Now, I am so harsh, but she sees the softness in it. I ask her, "How do you do it? With this much harshness, you spot very subtle softness." This is how it works. When we find the subtlety, the softness, in other's harshness, people get embarrassed and become soft. They cry, they ask for forgiveness.

This reminds me of the story of the sage and the master:

> One day a sage was thanking God. "You have helped to free my tribe. You have helped me by giving me wisdom to help my people."
>
> Then God said, "Yes, now that you have delivered your people, I want you to know that you are not wise enough. You can gain more wisdom."
>
> The sage said, "Thank you for telling me this, but how?"
>
> God said, "You have to go and find someone, one of my servants on Earth."
>
> "How will I know him?" the sage asked.
>
> God said, "Anywhere the dead become alive, he will be nearby."

So the sage searches everywhere for months and months and then, one day, he catches a fish to eat, but before he can eat it, the fish comes back to life and jumps out of his hand back into the water. Then he knows that the master is nearby. He looks around and sees an unknown, very mysterious man walking towards him.

"You have been looking for me, what do you want?" the man said.

The sage said, "God told me that you could help me gain wisdom."

The master said, "Listen, you can't gain it. Forget it and just go home."

The sage says, "No, I will really work hard. Help me!"

"Okay, I will give you three chances. All you have to do is travel with me. We will go to different places and at the right moment the lessons will come for you to see wisdom. If you miss three times, I can't help you."

So they traveled together until one day they came to a nice lake which they wanted to cross. There was a ferry there that took people to the other side, so they got on the boat. After they had crossed and were ready to leave, the ferryman said, "Listen, since you entered my boat, I feel like I am flying in the sky. I feel like I'm walking on clouds. Therefore, I don't want to charge you and your friend. It's free because you inspired me."

Right away the master took his walking stick and started hitting the bottom of the boat over and over again until he made a hole in the boat and it started sinking. Then the master hurried away. The ferryman was very angry and tried to catch the pair, but failed. The sage was shocked and thought, "My god what's wrong with this guy?! He's supposed to be a man of God!"

Then they got to a small town, a village, and the master took his stick and starting hitting a garden wall until he damaged it enough that the wall collapsed. Then he walked away. The sage thought the master was crazy. A little later, on the way out of the village, they saw a kid playing in the mud. The master walked up to the kid, cut his head off, and tossed it aside.

The sage said, "Wait a minute! Just wait one minute. This is crazy! I don't want to follow you. What in God's name are you doing?"

The master said, "Look, you missed three opportunities to gain wisdom. You don't understand anything that has happened, so I don't want to work with you either. You better leave and I'll go on my way."

The sage cried "What?! You've just been destroying everything."

The master said, "Listen, that boat, yes, I made a hole in it, but you didn't know that the next day the king of this country was going to war with the king of the neighboring country and that they would confiscate all the boats and all of them will burn and be destroyed. But this guy has a hole in his boat, so they can't take it because it will sink. He will fix his boat and soon he will be the only ferry carrying people back and forth across the lake. He will become rich because he didn't charge a man of God."

"The wall had a treasure inside, a pot of gold that a father had hidden there for a time when the family might need it in the future, but the father died before telling the sons that it was there. The sons really needed that money, otherwise they were going to lose their home to people they owed money to. So I broke the wall as the two sons were walking by. They saw the gold coming out of their garden wall, took it, and will pay the debt to save their home."

The sage said, "Well, what about the kid? You just killed a kid! What about that?"

"You still don't see the diamond in the rough. You don't. You just see the rough. You don't see the subtlety. You are not aware *that this kid was going to grow up and make war between two tribes and that there will be a lot of killing. I killed the kid, but, by his suffering, all of his karma got cleansed. His soul will go back to the womb of the same mother. She will have another child and when he grows up, he will become a peacemaker between the two tribes. He will be a beautiful person, but you don't see that." At this point, the master vanished. He became a light and left.*

To bring softness out from harshness, you have to become subtle yourself. Otherwise you will fall into the game and you will fight. This is what a mystic does or Existence does. Existence creates a harsh situation for the student. Then, in our sittings, I draw a subtlety out of this situation, and the student is touched deeply which causes their heart to open. They feel good. This is growth: high and low in order to grow.

If a person has a problem with harshness and if Existence wants to work with that person, then it will create many different, harsh situations for them. There is an old expression that says "Whatever you hate, that is what will happen to you," which really means these people are very dear to God and Existence is working with them. In fact, everybody is dear to Existence, but God works with the person who is ready to grow and go higher. If a person is not ready, Existence doesn't make unnecessary trouble for them.

Now, Farin, because you are ready, Existence works with you. For example, up until recently, your husband was harsh with you, but now he has changed and is soft. Existence wanted him to be harsh, so you could grow. Now that he is soft, some other person or situation will show up to be harsh. Even he can be tough again. But if you learn the lesson of how to deal with harshness and how to pull the softness from it, then, there would be no need for harshness around you anymore. Until then, Existence will hammer you on the head.

If you don't feel that you have learned this lesson, but still there is no harshness around you, there is a possibility that Existence is not working with you anymore. It says that you have done your growth to some level, so it is enough for this lifetime. But this will make you sad. You see now everything is one hundred eighty degrees different than we think. Instead of becoming upset because of some harshness, now you would be hurt for the lack of it.

FARIN: Which chakra is related to this problem with harshness?

SHARAM: In each chakra, it's different, but definitely if there are blockages in our fourth chakra *(the heart chakra)*, harshness will come to us. So harshness relates to the heart chakra and with you *(Farin)* it's so obvious. You need love around you. If there is no love, you will be disturbed. Mostly you get hurt by harshness because you wonder, why is there no love? Why is my heart closed now?"

THE DIAMOND IN THE ROUGH

The best of me,
The worst of me,
In your hands,
God's finest wine,
A diamond in the rough.

EVERYTHING HAS SPIRITUAL VALUE

SHARAM: *(In a conversation about punishment)* Punishment is something that I know everybody hates, but basically it tells us to do something for ourselves. Everything that Existence brings upon us has a spiritual value and if we understand that spiritual value, the pressure on us will be zero—the joy we feel will become a thousandfold. So this is how I work with people. As soon as I tell them the spiritual value of some negative thing that has happened, they become joyful. They become happy. They know that they are being worked on, they are being loved by Existence not hated by Existence. That's it.

*"Sometimes a shock,
or a strong poke is needed
to move us out of a stuck place.
It is with love that shock is given.
We just need to ask why was that shock necessary.
And any wounds arising from that shock…
Existence will take care of those too,
when the time is right,
but again don't forget to ask,
'Why is this new wound necessary
and why is it still here?'
When the benefits of that shock
or that poke descend on us,
then the wound will be healed."*

–Sharam

THE SUBTLETY OF LYING

FRANK: Why is it that there are people who lie and steal and do all sorts of negative things, but still their lives pass smoothly. They get whatever they want and nothing bad ever happens to them. Then, there are people who try to be good and they suffer to the end of their lives. In the end, they both die and before they are reborn Existence says, "Let's give everything to the one who lied and stole, to make his life better, and let's beat the hell out of the good guy to make his life harder.

SHARAM: Why would Existence do this? Look, what you are saying here is a lie. This is not true. You are lying without even knowing that you are lying. So you see, you also lie. Because you were claiming that you never lie.

FRANK: So this is not possible?

SHARAM: No. You see this is not possible, but your mind was saying that it was possible. So what you said was a lie and you didn't even know you were lying. So all these people that lie, they keep lying, but they don't know that they are lying.

It is that simple. You don't lie as grossly as others. Your lies are more subtle. People who lie don't know they are lying. It is hard for you to understand that. The mind has a delusion. It believes its own lies. All people are the same. Those who lie, forget that they are lying. Lying is a sickness. The person who lies is always deluding himself and can never come to the real world.

If you don't like someone lying, it shows that definitely you also lie, but you are not subtle enough to recognize your own lies. Maybe your lies are very subtle.

Also, a person who steals from others and lies will lose self-confidence. He has money that he has stolen, but no self-confidence.

I DESERVE

STREAM: I don't understand the connection between the feeling that I don't deserve and my fear that I'll look bad in front of people.

SHARAM: Nobody thinks that they *don't* deserve. There's no such thing. They just think that other people will not like them if they find out that they are not good enough. Everybody thinks, "I deserve everything." It's only in the group or in public that you think you don't deserve. When you are shy to talk in front of people in a sitting, it's the same thing. You worry that "I'll look bad," but our mind turns this around to "I don't deserve this." When you sit in the group or class and you are too shy to say something, you are too passive, you think that you don't deserve my time because other people are better than you. Why? They are better looking? They have more going for them? They know more? It comes from an inferiority complex, meaning inferior to someone else. "They are more superior, and I don't want to look bad. I don't want them to know what I know—that I'm not good enough. So I am going to be quiet, and I am going to be passive."

Do you see the connection?

STREAM: Yeah, it's pretty subtle.

SHARAM: Really, what it is, Stream, all these different words—jealousy, inferiority, superiority, looking bad, not deserving—these are all because we are looking superficially. We are looking at the surface. If you go deep to the roots, there is only one thing: EGO. And, if the ego steps aside you are in ecstasy. Agony or ecstasy, that's all there is. Misery or ecstasy.

STREAM: Is fear the same thing?

SHARAM: Same thing. What is fear? Afraid of losing, that's all. Fear means worrying about losing something. That comes from ignorance. You can't lose anything. We don't have anything. How can we lose it? There's nothing that we have.

You think you don't deserve. You don't deserve my love because you think you are not good enough. What is there to be good or not good? We are one with Existence. Can Existence be bad or good? No, it just is. You are beyond good and bad. Just Existence is. And Existence does what it does.

The interesting thing, Stream, is that everybody finds you interesting except you. Everybody really likes you.

When people don't like themselves, they go to two extremes: either they become aggressive or they become passive. I hope one day you start liking yourself, because if you like yourself, you will be assertive.

"When God is happy with you,
it is sheer nonsense
to be unhappy with yourself."

–Sharam

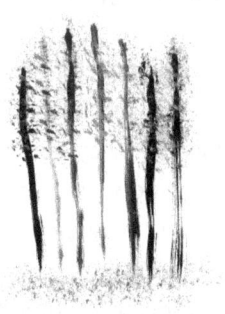

SEVEN CANDLES

CHRIS: I really have a need to connect with you. It worked out in class yesterday that whenever I looked at you, you were looking somewhere else. I started to fall into negativity. I got really miserable. You talked yesterday about the two paths, the path of love, those for whom connection with the teacher is most important, and the path of meditation, those who work more with meditation. I am on the path of meditation, so why do I fall apart if I don't have that connection with you?

SHARAM: There are two types of people: people who meditate and people who connect with the teacher. People who meditate have a small candle in all seven chakras. People who connect with the teacher have only one candle in the heart. If that candle in the heart really becomes big and bright, all the other chakras will become full of light too. People who have a candle in every chakra gradually have to meditate every day to make the candles bigger. Seven candles to light or only one candle to light. If you have only one candle, *everything* becomes a meditation. If you sleep, you are meditating because still you have the connection with the teacher. If you go to work, you are meditating. But for a meditator, they have to sit and meditate all the time.

But meditators need the connection too, because one of your seven candles is in the heart. On the days with no connection, the other candles get a good round. When you need time by yourself, you are working on the other candles. Only the heart needs the connection. The other candles need to be alone. They get connection with Existence, but then the mind comes in and says, "I'm separating myself. I'm not connecting with others. I'm out here by myself. Everybody is in there together." The mind has to understand that you are alone for a reason. Omar Khayyam, a great mystic, was alone a lot, sitting and watching the stars at night. Many mystics need that.

CHRIS: If I don't connect with your eyes, I don't feel like I'm connecting. Is that true?

SHARAM: Connection with the heart definitely comes with the eyes. The eyes are the door to the heart. That is very important, and I give plenty of opportunity for everyone to connect with me in this way, but some of my students don't have that option because they are not here with me. Out of necessity, they develop the same heart connection with the sound of my voice. It is like a blind person who eventually has to accept their blindness, and then their other senses become stronger. It will be the same for people who read this book. They will find a way to connect with me through these words too.

KHAYYAM

Beautiful lights glow brightly in here
Like stars in the heavens in sky so clear
One leading to son who speaks only of love
Constellation brighter brings God so near.

OUR PARTNER AS OUR UNCONSCIOUS

CHRIS: On anger: You said, in the past, I repressed anger, but now the anger is coming out. I get angry at my boyfriend a lot. Is that one of the reasons I have a relationship with him? So I have someone to fight with and get the anger out?

SHARAM: A woman's unconscious is male. A man's unconscious is female. The reason they get together and feel comfortable being with each other is because the woman reminds a man of his unconscious, and the man reminds the woman of her unconscious. Or, in other words, the woman feels comfortable with the man because the male of the man is more or less like the male of the woman in her unconscious, the male that she has repressed. And, vice versa.

The problems start after the honeymoon is over. If the woman is more female, it means she is hiding more of her male in her unconscious and because her male is in the unconscious, it means that she feels negatively towards the male side of herself. Then she starts having problems with the male outside. It is interesting that a more female woman most of the time will like a man with more male. This is to balance her 'more' femaleness with the 'more' maleness of a man. A woman that is stronger and has more male, she will like to be with a more gentle man.

So now, if there is an attraction between a man and a woman, it is because the man's unconscious, which is more female, recognizes itself in a woman on the outside, and that is why he's drawn to her. The same is true for the woman, her unconscious recognizes itself in the man. Initially the likenesses attract them to each other, but, then, these same likenesses create fight and anger and issues, because anything we have suppressed to the unconscious automatically means that, at some level, we didn't like it. And we have been suppressing these things, not only in this lifetime, but in past lifetimes too. After a while, in the relationship, the couple gets to know each other better, and as they do so, the woman starts looking almost exactly like the man's unconscious, so he begins to hate the woman and the woman begins to hate the man in the same manner. All of this is because they hate their own unconscious. He does a lot of things she can't stand. She does not know or cannot see the same things in herself because she has repressed them to the unconscious, but she can easily see it in him, so the fighting begins. The same happens for the man.

CHRIS: It seems like now we're fighting more than ever.

SHARAM: When things happen, in that moment, we always think it is worse than ever. Everyone does. When they get into their issues, they say this is worse than ever. Then they think, "I must be getting worse." It's not like that. When any negative thing is happening, we always feel that this is the worst it's ever been—just because it is negative. When the positive thing is happening, it is so positive that you say it is the best time of my life. We say that, but fighting is always worse. Believe me, no fighting can be better fighting. It is always worse.

Relation-sheep

(The pun refers to the idea that we all rush to relationship, playing established roles (not so different from children mimicking adults) in order to avoid rather than experience ourselves.)

"We all try to escape duality by getting into a relation-sheep, but when we find the opposite sex outside of ourselves, that duality gets worse. The distance between the male and the female becomes greater because we have placed the opposite sex further away from us (outside of us). When our own male and female connect, we get inner ecstasy. Not only that, but we can always count on our own male and our own female —you can take that to the bank. And remember: relationship is the greatest blessing to show us all these."

–Sharam

A COMET AND A DOVE

Single pointed arrow
Flaming through night
An arc of energy
Carving out light
As soft as the dawn
And as harsh
As desert light
Long past speed of sound
Overtaking that of light.

This comet colliding
With dove soft and still
Who happily rides tail
Of sweet Haley's will.
With the help of an angel
No longer fighting
Now god and goddess
Joyfully uniting.

Twice as fast
They move along
Together in love
Archer's arrow the pilot
Of giggling dove.

WHAT IS ANGER?

CHRIS: This repressed anger I have....

SHARAM: No, you didn't repress anger. You repressed negative energy, which comes out in the form of anger. Any time you express your negative feeling, we call that anger. If it is repressed, we don't call that anger. It will help us in the long run if we use the right terminology. This repressed energy that you have pushed inside is coming out in the form of anger.

CHRIS: Will this continue more and more?

SHARAM: It depends on us. The day you can see anger as negative energy and you can see it as it is piling up, when you can catch it in the moment and say to yourself, "Here it comes. Yes this is it. I feel it wanting to come out. I see I'm getting mad..., mad..., really mad." You see this, but because you are watching it, this negative energy doesn't become anger. It depends on how much you can watch it at the moment it is happening.

CHRIS: If I catch it at that point, will I get stuck in the negativity?

SHARAM: No, you won't.

CHRIS: Is catching the same as seeing it?

SHARAM: Yes, seeing is catching. The inner world is all about seeing. It is not about knowing, or doing. We often mistake these two—knowing and seeing. For example, with a spouse you say, "I know that he or she is going to make me mad again," but that doesn't help. You must see that you are boiling. You must see that this person is making you so mad in *this* moment. Then, you breathe deeply, about seven deep breaths, and you say to yourself, "I saw it before it happened. This man is exactly like my unconscious. The part I hate. Right now, this person is my unconscious standing in front of me acting crazy. No wonder I sent it to my unconscious. No wonder I hated it."

If you become one hundred percent conscious, you will never hate anyone.

CHRIS: I got angry at Baba *(one of the other students)* for a trivial issue. Instead of reacting I went outside to sit and be quiet. I was better when I finally came in. Is that catching it?

SHARAM: Yes. When we see something, we are experiencing it while at the same time watching it from a distance. Then we talk about it, like we are right now. All of this means working on yourself. A very effective catching is, first of all, not allowing more negative energy to pile up and second, when the negative energy wants to come in the form of anger, we look for the reason. In this case, it's that Baba was becoming your unconscious. It could be anyone with more male. It could be a woman. The female always has problems with the male, but neither the male nor the female will have a problem with someone whose male and female energies are balanced.

CHRIS: Overall, am I more male or more female?

SHARAM: I have seen you become more and more balanced throughout the years. You used to be more male. When you were more male, the female of other people bothered you more. You are becoming more female to balance your existing male.

DETOXING INSTEAD OF RETOXING

DEBBY: When I'm really emotional, I can't do anything. I couldn't even make a simple lunch for my husband this morning. This scares me a lot.

SHARAM: Over the years, we have cleansed the reservoir of repressed anger in you, and there is almost none left. Before, the repressed emotions could not come out because there was always anger.

Now, there are only emotions, which means the female was hiding underneath the male, before. The anger was the male. Today, the female has come out, and we are working on it directly.

Your crying is amazing. Today, you've gotten to all that repressed emotion, and when you get there so much energy gets lost that you can't do anything else. You can't even pack a lunch, because you are cleansing immensely.

You are detoxing instead of "retoxing." When the anger came up before, you would retox. Today you are detoxing the emotions.

You are working on yourself. Who cares about lunch? How many times in past lifetimes have you prepared lunch to give to your husband to take to work? Too many times and it amounted to nothing. Today you are cleansing your emotional body and you will get rid of it for eternity.

You don't even have to become enlightened. If you clean your emotional body, that's it—forever. If you ever come back again, in your next lifetime, it will be all clean and ready to go. You will have no emotional issues for all eternity. What a relief! Nothing is more important than what you are doing.

The interesting thing is that with crying, we gradually clean the emotional body, but with acceptance, we knock a huge chunk out of the emotional body. We bring the element of acceptance in by understanding that making lunch is not important. Cleaning the emotional body by crying is important. We begin to accept it.

If we only cry, we cannot clean the emotional body in one lifetime. If we have acceptance, we can clean the emotional body in a few days. Crying alone needs maybe four lifetimes. If you bring total acceptance to it while you are crying, it can take a few days.

Let's say the whole emotional body is cleansed. The female is perfectly clean, balanced, rounded, and ready to go. First of all, you can't get to the female unless your male is cleaner and the anger is gone. Then if you clean the emotional body, you go right to the heart; you become a pir. Pir means someone who is not enlightened yet, but is just below enlightenment.

SAY "CHEESE"

RABIA: I hate having my picture taken. I always look so ugly and I don't want pictures to reflect that. Is it because I have so much karma?

SHARAM: You think you are ugly not because of yourself—you think other people think you are ugly. So ugliness or beauty has nothing to do with you. You always picture yourself looking ugly for others. That's why the camera bugs you, because the photos will show to the world and to yourself that you are ugly. Our sense of beauty or ugliness comes from the eyes of others. Otherwise you don't care how you look. If nobody is around, you look sloppy, you don't care. You only want other people to think you are beautiful. So if that is what you want, instead of wasting energy worrying and wondering, just go and check with them. Ask them, "Am I beautiful or not?" You are making yourself suffer all the time. When you look in the mirror, you suffer unnecessarily. Do you see how unnecessary this is?

EVERYTHING IS PERFECT

SHARAM: I was on the phone last Monday with the people overseas, including Hafez. He left the villa after the class was over and he started coughing. He got sick and threw up. Then, he fell. He was under a tree. It was evening. It was dark. And then he said he had a big realization.

HAFEZ: I realized that every moment God, Existence has created, has engineered, so nicely, so perfectly. And what do we do? We mess it up by wanting to change things, by not liking what is happening, by thinking we have to do something else, by controlling it, bringing so much third chakra in it. If we just relax and know that this moment, every moment is perfect, why would we ever want to do anything to change it?

This is God. God has created this. How can I do better? This is perfect. If we understand this, we will be so relaxed.

SHARAM: He decided from there on, he would be happy with everything. Nothing will bother him. Every moment, every second is perfect. Why would he need to get involved in it? And this is a sixteen-year-old. He really meant it. It was so perfect. He said since Monday, which was a few days ago, nothing bothers him. He said he saw the light in that moment. Something popped, something opened up and he's just so happy.

He jumped to the heart. The third chakra wants to control everything, which means the third chakra kills Existence, but everything is just perfect all the time.

Basically, what Hafez is doing right now is saying there is no good and no bad. Nothing is good. Nothing is bad. Everything is transformative, all the time.

If you don't realize, if you are really asleep and you don't have any inkling of awareness, then you are part of this whole game. You are suffering and that is perfect. Once you start to gain awareness—when you are no longer totally unaware, nor are you totally "let go"—you cannot go back to not knowing that you are suffering. You have to make a jump.

All you have to do is one jump and not worry about anything because everything is Existence's doing—everything except your worrying. Worrying falls under the category of a person's free will. Anyone else's worrying, doing, thinking; you can't do anything about that. You have free will inside, but not outside. How can you stop the night? Now it's night. You can't stop it. You can't say don't become dark. It's a force. How can I tell Jerry, you have to become enlightened right now? He might try, but I cannot force him.

You have free will for yourself and yourself only. The third chakra tries to control the outside. "Everybody should listen to everything I say. I am the boss," but its efforts are futile.

SWEET, SWEET SONS

Thank you sweet, sweet sons
Thank you for the day
Thank you for that smile
As you passed along the way
Thanks for teaching me to listen
Thanks for crying so I could see
Thanks for all the joy you've brought me
and for teaching me about me
Thanks for peeing out the window
When the bathroom's three steps away
Thanks for jumping off the roof
Laughing all the way
Thanks for refusing to budge
So I could learn to give way
Oh, and thanks for teaching your friends
To also pee that way
Thanks for not being perfect
In front of grandma and granddad
And for always being yourself
Forcing me to reevaluate good and bad
I'm not thanking you for what you say
Or even what you do
Just thanking you for all I feel
When I am off with you.
Each response is slightly different
Simple and complex
All helping me to see myself
And ending ego's hex.

THE GOOD AND BAD OF GUILT

FARIN: How is guilt created? Is it a conditioning?

SHARAM: Guilt is one of the branches of negative feelings that are in our unconscious and, yes, guilt is just a conditioning. When you were a kid, you were told, "Don't do that." Now, when you do that, you feel guilty. So guilt means repressed negative feelings that show themselves as regret, and usually it started with the word "bad." It starts with one of the many of times when we were told something is bad. If you don't think in terms of bad, then you will have acceptance and you will never regret anything. When you have acceptance, you won't repress anything, therefore you won't feel guilty and you won't get angry. We get angry because we don't have acceptance.

Expectation is the same. Expectation is also related to good and bad. We expect people to behave in a way that we consider good. So you see it goes back to good and bad. Or when we compare, we say this is good and that is bad. So comparison is based on good and bad.

But if we don't think of good and bad, we won't compare, we won't judge, and we will feel free, total freedom. All the sufferings are because of this stupid good and bad. All judgments, all comparisons, guilt, anger, not accepting. If we put good and bad aside, we will live in heaven.

ENERGY, THE MIND, AND THE MOMENT

We had a class that wasn't very strong. We did some breathing exercises and it became very strong.

SHARAM: Often in these classes, I spend time reading or we talk, but the moment, any moment, is not about talking. The moment is about putting your mind aside. When I talk to you, it is only to bring understanding to your mind so it stops. There is a sudden silence, a moment of "Aha!" when a topic hits home for you. Then all of a sudden, the mind stops. It goes into ecstasy. The mind can stop in two ways. Either it slows down so much that you fall asleep or it goes to the heights of understanding, and then it stops. My sitting here is about your mind stepping aside, so you can experience unity with the whole, with Existence.

Why stop the mind? Your inside and your outside want to come together. Right now they try, but this thing called the mind is in between. When the mind steps aside, then you experience yourself with Existence as one. This is what is good for you. That's the only reason you are here, not only here in this room, but also here on Earth.

Everything else is secondary. Everything else is nonsense. And we focus on nonsense for so long, all the time.

CLEAR VOICE TO SING

A mind dry and dusty
Filled with dry rot
Hell bent on worrying
Trust me, A lot!!!
Then I come here
To my circle of friends
And slowly light enters
As suffering ends
Cocoon bursts open
With giggling delight
Revealing beautiful butterflies
Of color so bright
Tentative brush of wing
Then an explosion of flutter
Clear voice to sing
Only Love to utter.

THE PEACEMAKER

A situation came up in which Sharam was honest with Shahed about something in a way that she felt was harsh and hurtful. He was very direct. He said, "What, I can't be honest with you?" It made her realize all the ways in which she felt that she couldn't be honest with others, especially when she was angry with them or had something negative to say. She felt that she had become very political in her dealings with people—that she was afraid people would get angry with her if she expressed her feelings directly.

SHARAM: Shahed, you need your fear. You need to be political. Otherwise others' egos will fry you. In being political, you screen the stuff you don't need while the stuff you need filters through the screen. All because of your fear. Don't be afraid of your fear because it is helping you immensely. Otherwise, Existence wouldn't have it there. Don't be afraid of your fear; you need it. Absolutely, it is necessary.

SHAHED: So why do I need to screen? For example, Debby doesn't need to screen as much as I do.

SHARAM: Okay, very good question. Debby doesn't need it because she is a different person. She has had a totally different life than you.

If you had the same background as Debby, you wouldn't need it as much either. There is a saying that says, "There are as many paths to God as there are people on Earth."

SHARAM: *(To Debby)* How many sisters and brothers do you have?

DEBBY: One brother, and I was the oldest.

SHARAM: *(To Shahed)* You got it, right there. You have four brothers, older and younger, so you needed to be political.

SHAHED: I just feel like I'm ... maybe a liar is too strong of a word, but, I'm just not direct. I go all around what I want to say. Have I become so political that I've lost the ability to be straight forward?

SHARAM: You bring gentleness to the situation. You work in a way that doesn't harm others. You are a peacemaker, don't call yourself political. Jesus talked about this a lot, peacemakers and heaven. *("Blessed are the peacemakers for they will be called sons of God" Mathew 5.9).*

Next day

SHAHED: I feel frustrated when I am angry because, at those times, a lot of mind and thinking come up around how to express my feelings and whether or not I should express that anger at all. Two nights ago, I was in a situation I didn't like, but I couldn't express that I didn't like it. Today, I feel physical and emotional pain.

SHARAM: When something negative happens and we cannot do anything about it, that negativity stays with us for a long time, unless we have a way to get rid of it. That's why an active meditation would be good for you. Maybe shaking, or screaming while hitting a pillow.

SHAHED: You told me that frustration is anger that is not moving out towards others nor inwards towards ourselves. It is just sitting there. I noticed that during our last active meditation, all I could feel was frustration. I couldn't get it to move.

SHARAM: You needed the stuff that happened two nights ago to get it out. When anger is not so much, then it doesn't come out, it doesn't go in. We get frustrated, but if there is more anger, then it will come out. It is gone. Or we can move the negative energy with some understanding.

I used to be very forward and talkative, but when I started to go deeper and deeper into myself, all of the sudden, I was not that way anymore. I was awkward in society. I was shy and couldn't talk. Before, I could speak my mind, but when I went deeper, there was a period of time when I couldn't speak my mind. I couldn't say anything. With people I was so shy. I thought that wasn't good, but later on I found out what was happening to me. If someone talks about mysticism you will talk; you will be happy. You are becoming more subtle and things that are not subtle are becoming disagreeable to you. Before it was not agreeable, but you would fight. Today it is not agreeable, and you can't and won't fight. You don't say anything and you feel uncomfortable. "Why don't I say anything?" Because I have been through this and understand where you are right now, I think, "Oh, that's great. She's much more advanced now," but you are in it, so it is a big thing.

SHAHED: I feel like I'm so false when I am talking to some of my old friends, people who are not on the path. I feel so out of my element. I feel insecure and not as good as them.

SHARAM: What is happening is that gradually we see what is our real element. You will see that you are uncomfortable for some good reason. When you jump at yourself and say why did I say that? Why was I dishonest? You don't stop and answer yourself. You just punish yourself. You should answer yourself. Why am I dishonest? If you look for an answer it will come. The answer is, there is no other way to be around these people. If you're honest, everybody gets hurt. There will be complications. Too much breaking society's rules and unnecessary pain. Everybody becomes enemies. Then you learn that there are two ways of being dishonest, one for good reasons and one for bad reasons, kosher, not kosher, helpful, not helpful. Why am I dishonest? If we are honest the world becomes unlivable. Nobody can live on Earth. Then you can't even call it dishonesty. You call it workability with people. Get away from the word you didn't like. Then you will be at ease.

SHAHED: What I see is that sometimes I get a message from Existence loud and clear, but I don't follow it. Like the situation I was in a couple days ago, I knew I should have avoided it all together, but I went with the rules of society—the rules that say a good mother should go. Existence was practically hitting me in the face with don't go, but I didn't follow it.

SHARAM: Then again the love of Existence is this. You went to the meeting so that you could hear the things that were said here today or so that you could learn something. It is perfect. Everything that happens in Existence is so superbly amazing. It's just beautiful.

ROOM FOR IMPROVEMENT

SHARAM: *(Talking about Stream's crying)* When you cry, you get sympathy. You get rough edges, get hard, then I call you on it—then you want to cry. This is a passive way to grow. You might cleanse a little bit, but mostly you just get sympathy. It's a good racket.

STREAM: Well, that's bad. Now I feel I don't have any worth. So, again I've put it *(my self-worth)* back on you.

SHARAM: You caught yourself!

STREAM: But I'm doing something wrong. I've got a racket going; I'm no good, and I hide it. I have no value, no worth.

SHARAM: What do you mean by value?

STREAM: Value is being authentic. It's bad to run a racket.

SHARAM: Why do you call it bad? Why don't you call it room for improvement? You call it bad, and the space becomes really weak. You feel like I scold you. All I mean is I see a racket, let's work on it.

I say you're passive; let's understand passivity. Let's situate you in the picture. Let's open that, let's understand deeper. What does Stream do? What you understand is, "I'm no good." What you do is cry. You make the space weak, bring sadness to the space. You constantly go into, "I'm not good."

You must be crazy not to change it! You want to fight? Who? Why not change? I'm pulling you out of this frame of mind: You think, "I did my life. My life is over. I'm ready to die. I can't change." You thought your life is over. Today there is a new beginning. So, I constantly have to pull you out of it.

STREAM: Interesting....

SHARAM: When you say interesting, it has energy of death and coming out of death. It has a big, heavy death energy—just the way you said it, and just the word "interesting." I'm constantly pulling you and you are resisting.

SELF-WORTH

Following Stream's sitting on self worth or rather the lack of it, Livia asked about her destructive thoughts when she is depressed and wants to give up.

LIVIA: Why do I even go to destructive thoughts when I'm depressed?

SHARAM: You forget that you want to be one with Existence before you depart.

You say you don't want to suffer anymore. The same thing happens with Stream or other people. Something goes wrong, something doesn't go the way you think is right and then you go to negative thoughts, the ultimate of which is the one where you want to leave your body, to die. We think death is an avenue that we can escape to. We only have these thoughts because we are not ready to look at the issue at hand. We don't want to take responsibility.

LIVIA: My despair, though, stems from having too many issues to work on. There are so many, it seems hopeless.

SHARAM: That's not really the case, because we never know how the process may evolve. By breaking one frontier, others may just follow in succession. We just never know. Just look at the heaviness, see what's there, and go forward.

EYES TO SEE

Oh where or where could my love be?
If only my heart had eyes to see
Then I would always know
He's here with me.

ACCEPTANCE

CHRIS: Condemnation and lack of acceptance helps push me to work on myself. How do I get acceptance for myself when the lack of acceptance is what is pushing me to work on myself?

SHARAM: By understanding and knowing that when condemnation and non-acceptance are no longer necessary, they will disappear by themselves.

CHRIS: Okay.

SHARAM: You see, you just said okay. As soon as you understood, you said okay. Okay means acceptance. Every time you understand something, you accept. You come here to understand, which will lead to acceptance. People that are not working on themselves don't understand. They just live life and condemn themselves all the time. They don't do anything about it, because they don't understand. Somehow you came here and understood something, and you stayed longer and you understood more, and you understood more. Here you understand more, which leads to self-acceptance.

Right now you are accepting yourself. That is why you are smiling. This moment is a part of your life where acceptance is happening.

When you want to leave your body, you will say, "I had so many sittings with Sharam and so many acceptances and that was wonderful." You've had lots of wonderful sitting time and understanding time, so you are building up your life with acceptance. Then you go home from here and your mind comes in and you start doubting this and that, and questioning things. For example, you say, "I'm not good enough." Then, tomorrow, you come back and sit here and again we open up some issues. If this happens many times, at one point, magic will happen. You will do a jump. That's what we call transformation—transformation that, at one point, will become the ultimate jump to enlightenment.

Remember, every time we talk about something, right away you go, "Wow, yes, yes." You go to acceptance. If you add up all the acceptances you have had here with me, that in itself is a chunk of your life, a chunk where you are living happily. We tend to forget to count the here and now as part of life. Imagine, there are people who never accept themselves or their lives, and who don't get the time that you get in understanding and acceptance. They rarely, if ever, get to experience the joy that understanding brings. You experience this almost daily. With deeper understanding, all of a sudden, you will come to total acceptance forever, for eternity.

CHRIS: I can see that I am getting better at catching myself from falling into the negativity. When I do fall now, I seem to fall really hard and fast. Do I inevitably still have to go to negativity or is it different now?

SHARAM: If you catch yourself, you won't go to negativity. Sometimes what happens happens so fast that you can't catch it, so you need to become even more skillful in catching yourself. Becoming more skillful in catching means becoming more aware through meditation, deep breathing, and all the work we do here. To become more aware means to become more open, more sensitive, more accepting, more centered, more wise, and more loving.

Give yourself a couple of years. Give yourself some time. Becoming a doctor takes several years. Becoming Godlike might take a little longer—or a little shorter. You are aiming to be one with the highest, with the whole universe.

EXPLOSION OF LOVE

Our hearts are so full of love,
They're like ticking time bombs
Beating away in our chests
Ready to explode at the slightest provocation:
A look, an offer of a stranger's hand,
A father really listening to what a son has to say;
And
Kabam! Kablooey! Kapow!
That heart knocks the other right off their feet
Like a tidal wave.
No wonder we're so afraid of love.
But fear not fellow travelers and
You will surf that wave
Like you've never surfed before,
Riding the backs of dolphins,
Flipping, twisting, and diving
Willing to risk total annihilation
In the wake of your beloved.

THE NEW APARTMENT

JERRY: We had decided it was time to get our own place, but before, when we talked to you about it, it was always in the back of my mind, that we couldn't do it. I kept thinking, "We can't move to a house totally of our own. We've had roommates for so long and we have no rental history or even a recent payment history of paying the utilities and other bills. We only have two weeks to get out. I just kept telling myself that it was not going to happen. But, then, after we talked to you, it happened.

SHARAM: That saying in the back of the mind of, "It's not going to happen," creates it not to happen. But when you and I sat here, on a previous sitting, and I said it was really good because Cindy needs a place to stay, two things went into your subconscious. The first was, "I definitely will be helping someone," and the second was, "Sharam is okaying it, so it's going to happen." Your trust, your belief, and your faith made it happen.

JERRY: I stopped worrying about it not happening after we had that sitting.

SHARAM: That shows that you have faith, and that's a great thing to have. Better than anything else. It doesn't matter what you have, if you have many cars, if you have money, if you have beauty, it doesn't matter. If you don't have faith, you are poor. And if you have faith and you don't have anything else, then you are rich. And you do have faith. It doesn't matter how many times your subconscious says, "No, it cannot happen." If you have faith, when someone you really believe in and trust says it will happen, then you make it possible. When you trust and have faith in me, that doesn't mean that I am important. The more faith you have, the more important you are. It's about you, not anybody else. All the magic and all the miracles happen because of you.

JERRY: It seems you help us in the "faith" department.

SHARAM: I help the people that already have it; I help to bring it out. My help is just giving a tap on the head and the faith wakes up. Some people don't have faith. It won't matter what I do, they still will not have it. How do you make a miracle? No matter what your subconscious tells you, when you have that faith, and trust what I say, no matter what it is, you do it and get it done. It feels like a miracle. It takes effort to do things, but when you have faith, everything becomes easy. No matter how much effort it takes or difficulties you go through, it all seems easy with faith. When the heart opens, things get done.

This moment, the connection is the most important thing because you totally come to the here and now. These moments pile up and are the only things you'll have when you leave your body. You can't take anything with you. The only things you carry with you are these moments of intense connection, heart to heart. That's the only thing that you have.

WHO IS RESPONSIBLE FOR WHAT?

FARIN: God puts our ego aside. We don't have to worry about it. God makes it happen.

SHARAM: That is the most stupid thing I've ever heard! Ecstasy, love, and compassion all happen, but *we* have to put our ego aside. It's the only thing we have to do on this Earth, the only thing. Everything else happens. You don't want to take responsibility. It's egoistic to think like that. Your ego is the only thing that God will not touch out of respect for you, because it's either your ego or God. So you have to do something about your ego. You have to put it aside. If you do so, everything else will be given to you.

IF THE EGO WINS, WE LOSE

SHARAM: If the ego wins, we lose. If we win, ego loses. The ego's loss is our gain.

Ego is a generic term for pride, for the fact that we think we are the most important thing or person in the whole world. When there is ego, we need to protect it because ego is very fragile. With the smallest thing, it falls apart. Because of this quality, we are prone to have fear—fear of breaking down, fear of losing our grip on life. But when the ego is lost, for the first time we can breathe the breath of freshness, with no fear, no anxiety, no worries. Then we are present, each moment, to experience what is happening right now.

Ego gains power in fighting because there is no let-go in fighting. If we let go, really we are letting the ego go, so the ego likes to fight with others. It cannot live without fighting. On the other hand, only in letting go and allowing, only in our acceptance, is there no ego. When we surrender to God, there is no ego.

SNORING

LEILA: Why have I started to snore?

Sharam had told Leila that husbands and wives shouldn't sleep in the same room. In this sitting, he explains why.

SHARAM: *(To Leila)* You are a good girl. You listen to the me. Because I told you to sleep in a different room and you didn't, your subconscious is causing you to snore.

When you sleep, you are totally unconscious. We don't want to give our unconscious to anyone else. Sleeping is symbolic.

You should hold your unconscious for yourself, but offer your conscious to your spouse. This is very loving, subtle, and advanced.

When you die, you don't die together. You leave this world alone. Sleep is like death, so sleep alone. In the morning you join together.

THINKING VERSUS AWARENESS

TORRY: We said that thoughts are like the leaves of the tree, but the need for thinking was the roots. You can try to cut the leaves, but the roots will just grow more. For example, I was thinking, you can lose weight, but if the reason for being overweight is still in the subconscious, you will just get fat again. Then you said awareness cuts the need for thinking from the roots, and the leaves fall away. So how does awareness relate to thinking or reduce the need for thinking?

SHARAM: As long as you need the thinking, the thinking goes on. When awareness replaces the thinking, the thinking stops. Awareness is so high. Awareness is so powerful that when it comes, the leaves will fall off by themselves.

If you want to stop thinking—if, while you are meditating, you are focused on trying to stop the mind, the thoughts—it doesn't work. Sometimes the thinking even gets worse.

TORRY: I know.

SHARAM: Instead, let's meditate to grow awareness. We become aware of our breathing or we are aware of our thoughts, but we don't become involved in them. In doing so, our awareness grows. As the awareness grows, the thinking slows. And when there's a lot of awareness, all of a sudden, there's no need for thinking. You've got the diamond. There's no need for thinking any more. You totally stay in the moment all the time. That means feeling lots of love, lots of ecstasy. When I say ecstasy, you really don't know what I'm talking about.

TORRY: Awareness is a wonderful concept. I haven't gotten my mind around it yet.

SHARAM: We don't want your mind around it. *(Uproarious laughter)*

TORRY: Oh God. I'll get this someday, won't I? This is hard for me.

SHARAM: The reason this is hard for you is because it's so easy. It's the easiest thing. You don't need to wash dishes or do anything. That's why it's hard for you. You know doing. If there were certain things to be done, you could do them. But this is not about doing anything. It's the easiest thing. What I'm really saying is that you are perfect as you are right now. You will get it someday, but you don't get it right now.

TORRY: You keep saying it, and I don't get it.

SHARAM: So how can we gain more chaos in your life? All your life you've been trying to put things in order.

TORRY: Control, plans, the whole nine yards....

SHARAM: We think chaos is bad. Then, on the path of mysticism, all of a sudden we say everything is chaos. Chaos is God.

TORRY: Well, I can stop trying to control and plan as much.

SHARAM: That's very controlling, if you want to stop controlling.

TORRY: Okay, well, do you have suggestions?

SHARAM: Just hold my hand. *(lots of group laughter)*

TORRY: *(Holding Sharam's hands)* I'm getting hot and nervous.

SHARAM: That's what we call chaos. *(more laughing)*

(Torry hugs Sharam.)

SHARAM: See how much better things got?

TORRY: My controlling and planning have been driving my husband nuts. Just to let you know.

SHARAM: It's been driving me nuts, too. *(More laughter)*

TORRY: I know. So I need to let go and enjoy the ride?

SHARAM: This is something we have to do all the time.

TORRY: I know. I know. I'm trying to figure that out. But I'm perfect right now?

SHARAM: Even if you are controlling, it is perfect right now.

TORRY: Really?

SHARAM: Yes, because if you really accept your controlling, you will go above and beyond it. You see, right now, you control and you hate it. You used to hate it subconsciously, but now, gradually, this controlling has become more conscious and you don't like it. If you say, this is the way I am, you will accept it. Acceptance is higher than controlling. If you really accept it, then you will go to the heart. Every time you accept something, it's so high it sends you right to the heart. At the right moment, the controlling will go away. Right now is not the right moment.
　Thank you. I love you very much.

TORRY: I love you too.

SHARAM: That "thank you" didn't mean that the sitting is ending. I am not controlling this sitting.

TORRY: You talked about going to the two poles, like eating or fasting. I either control or say forget it, step back, and absolutely, positively do nothing except worry.

SHARAM: Oh my God. That is doing a lot. Worrying is a lot. It takes so much energy. I see that you are smiling right now. Are you enjoying this moment?

TORRY: I am very much enjoying this moment. These moments make it all worthwhile *(begins to cry)*. Thank you very much, Sharam.

PERIODS, SELF-CONFIDENCE, AND TOOTING YOUR OWN HORN

SHAHED: My question is why does my self-confidence plummet during my period, you know, a couple of days before and the first day or two of it?

SHARAM: This is the nature of periods. This is the nature of it. Your centeredness falls apart. That's the chaos part of the whole thing. During your period, you fall apart, you're not centered anymore. Then afterwards, you become more integrated, more together. This is a wonderful way for women to absolutely grow. So it's perfect. It's God's gift to women. They become much wiser. Chaos and then order comes and then again chaos each month. Wow!

SHAHED: Sometimes, I'd just like to go away every month for two or three days and not have to deal with my life during this time. I feel so overwhelmed and that I suck at everything. Everything just goes ppphhht. Do I just keep going on with my life and feel the chaos?

SHARAM: You go with whatever you feel, whatever you want to do. It's perfect because if you force it and say, "No, I shouldn't do this; I should do whatever I'm *supposed* to do," versus whatever you really want to do, you're trying to amend the chaos, make it better. But you really have to go with chaos, the spontaneous feelings, so you can grow deeper when you come back out of it.

SHAHED: When I'm in it, in terms of the world, it's very difficult. In terms of intuition, it's a great time. Most women hate their periods, but I look forward to it every month. Is that weird?

SHARAM: That's wonderful that you are looking forward to it. There's a higher thing in you that you're getting in touch with more and more. It's beyond the mind. The mind is a little thing. The inner understanding, your soul, is much, much, much, much greater. So more and more, you are getting in touch with your soul and it tells you, it gives you an inclination, a feeling that this period is good. Up to now, the mind didn't know exactly why, but that feeling was there. That's why you were looking forward to it, you wanted it, because of that feeling in the back, way back of your being. Now, today, your mind understood it too. So now, it just leaves you alone. It will be really fun.

SHAHED: Thank you. Gosh, you're just amazing.

SHARAM: That's what I feel about you.

SHAHED: I feel amazing right now about me too, just because I was going to come up here and start crying about all the things that I feel like I can't do anymore and then at the very end I thought no, that's not the issue here. I feel kind of bad for tooting my horn, but I was so excited when I realized the question is about losing my self-confidence during my period, not all the things I've temporarily lost my confidence over.

SHARAM: But I love when you toot your horn. It's beautiful. Because it's true. You're not tooting on some hot air—it's real. And you know we've been misled—we've been told you'll get a big ego, so watch for that—don't toot your horn—don't say good things about yourself. This is misleading. When there is something real, you have to say it.

Otherwise you lose that self-confidence. There is a fine line between self-confidence and having an ego. You won't gain self confidence if you have fear of getting ego. Watch for that. If you do something which is really good, don't worry about it. Just mention it.

"We build self-confidence to drop it."

–Sharam

WORRY AND SEIZURES

JEANNETTE: Last Sunday you mentioned that I had not had any seizures or preliminaries *(symptoms that come before a seizure, but don't always result in a seizure)* and I agreed. However, on Tuesday, following that sitting, the preliminaries started in. On Wednesday, I had a seizure just before class on the carpet outside the classroom. I believe I was scared that Jerry was going back to work last Tuesday.

SHARAM: When you pay attention to something, you give it food. When I bring it to your attention that you haven't had a seizure, the subconscious mind says, "Oh, I forgot to have seizures." Basically, what it means is that this seizure is nothing. You're much bigger now. You have control over it. Only when you give in to it, when you feel weak or you feel female, it happens. When you become more balanced, it never happens.

JEANNETTE: Also, my attachment to Jerry is very strong and, when I am in a situation where my surroundings are changed, even a little, I go to my emotional body.

SHARAM: If you are in the second chakra, you go to the emotional body. If you are in the first chakra, your subconscious thinks that nothing can be done, there is no hope. The seizure is telling you that you are allowing something to be bigger than you. You feel there is something that is too big for you to handle, for example, when Jerry went back to work, you felt you couldn't handle it yourself. You couldn't get attention by doing something because he *has* to go back to work, so the attention comes with a seizure. But this time you didn't try to get attention, you didn't say anything in the class, so it is getting healthier. It is gradually leaving you, because you don't want to give attention to it.

JEANNETTE: I seem to worry about things even though I don't know I'm worrying about them.

SHARAM: When you worry, right away you start not wanting to worry, so you're worrying and fighting the worrying all at the same time. Worrying, in itself, takes so much of your energy that automatically you fight it because you don't like that loss of energy. But not liking the worrying or fighting the worrying also takes up a lot of energy. So between the two, you fall into the lowest part of you because of this lack of energy, which, in your case, means preliminaries or seizures. The preliminaries are really a gift for you because they cause you to worry *more*. You think, "A seizure might be coming." This way your worrying becomes more **total** and you become aware of it. That awareness brings you to the moment. You get fresh juice (energy) which in return, brings you higher and you to go back to your regular, healthy life.

So the preliminaries actually help you. They cause you not to go lower and the fight and worrying stops, and all of a sudden you have more energy and you don't fall to the bottom. There is nothing more worth living for than expanding yourself. Existence keeps us alive for no other reason.

TWO ANGELS

Touched by a master
Blessed he is near
But kept at a distance
By past parents' fear
Hearts that are longing
Threatening to arise
Unable to resist
Sweet Master's eyes

INNER DIALOGUES

SHARAM: When you don't have unity among each other, when you don't feel connected with someone, when you are still separate, you start having inner dialogues with them. So every time you have an inner dialogue, you feel separate from someone. This inner dialogue leads to blaming, you blame the other. Right away when you blame someone, you start suffering and that suffering makes you angry. Or you might go to sadness. When a lot of that happens you feel depressed. This is a vicious circle. All the time it happens. So know whenever you catch yourself having an inner dialogue with someone, it is just because you have separated yourself from them.

SECOND CHAKRA

SHARAM: If your second chakra is closed, you are not centered; you want to put your center outside yourself, so you constantly look for someone to say, "Hey you're great, you're good, I like you." You want affirmation, approval. You want them to tell you that you are a good person. Remember, when you don't have your second chakra open, then you need affirmation from outside. When you have your second chakra open you have centeredness—whatever happens, you are happy. If they adore you, you love it; if they don't, it doesn't make a difference, still you love it. That's one issue of the second chakra.

SEEING THE MASTER

When on the path of mysticism we find someone to guide us through our inner journey, we call that person a spiritual teacher. Other paths use other terms like master, guru, etc.

SHARAM: Being in the presence of a master can be a life changing phenomenon. If you are open and ready to receive his energy, there is the possibility of the heart opening. In other words, the energy travels all the way to the higher chakras creating joy and ecstasy. But if you are filled with ego, you will feel bad, yucko, because whenever you are with him, automatically you are burning your ego. You are burning karma and remember, karma feels the same way coming out as it did going in.

RESIST NOT

SHARAM: *(To Mahsa)* We learned to resist when we were young because our parents and teachers and others wanted us to do things that we didn't want to do. We learned to resist because they wanted to give us shots and we didn't want them. They wanted us to eat when we wanted to play. Gradually we learned to resist. As people grow older, they give even less space to others. They always watch to see what the other is doing and they judge all the time.

First we have to see we are resisting, then tell ourselves we are resisting, and finally, tell ourselves to stop it.

THE HIGHWAY

The next time you catch yourself
About to spout
"It's my way or the highway."
Clap your hand over your mouth
Turn around and run,
As fast as you can
Until you chase that thought
Right out of your head.
Cause they'll choose the highway
They have to
It's the only route
To their soul.

HEAVEN OR EARTH

BABA: Why do souls reincarnate on Earth?

SHARAM: There is light, a huge globe of light. This is God. Now some small part of this light travels to Earth and obeys Earth's laws by entering a woman's body and becoming a baby. Baba has asked about an enlightened person, but everybody does the same. All of you guys did the same thing.

So this light comes down from the source and all of a sudden parents have a child. The name is not Sharam, or Livia, or Tom, but God. We just change it. Originally, God doesn't have a name; it's just the source, but we get this idea that we have to name our son or daughter.

This light came for a mission, to make sure that Existence grows. You come down here and your mission is to grow. Your mission is to bring two opposite poles close to each other, to merge them, to go above and beyond them, to transform, to grow. That's why we are here, to grow. Because, when you grow you enjoy. It adds to the ecstasy of Existence. Otherwise Existence will be dead. Existence always wants to have a little more ecstasy. Is that greedy of Existence? Maybe. Greedy for more joy.

We come because we are all on a mission from Existence. You come from a mother's womb and you grow up and then, at one point, you're mature enough that you're ready to do your mission. *(In Sharam's case the mission is to help others.)* Actually, for all of us, it's the same thing—to grow—except some people get so much involved with mediocre things, daily things, that they forget they have a mission here. Billions don't know. Millions know, but don't have time to do it or they just don't know what to do. Very few say, "growth is why I came here."

There are many things on Earth that we can get involved with and forget our mission. The best is money. Others are power and expanding the mind. Your mind is a computer with a lot of memory cells. Room in the mind can be used for true intelligence. For instance, someone who doesn't go to college is called dumb by society, but society is wrong. This person has more space, more unused memory for real intelligence. Empty space in your brain means you are intelligent. Like a young child, you are more available to the moment. Otherwise, you are a scholar. A scholar is someone who develops their mind, but the mind is simply a collection of ideas and memories stored from the past to be projected onto the future. If you have more brain cells that are empty, then you are a mystic. Mystic means someone who is alive. A scholar means someone who is dead. Alive means flowing and totally in the moment. Dead means you are like a rock, you have a big ego. The scholar misses this moment.

For the enlightened person, Existence makes a decision that this is the time for this soul to go back, not so much to grow, but to help others to grow, but meanwhile the enlightened person grows too.

Why is there Earth? Here, people get confused, but if they're confused and still find the real thing, then it means even more. That's the only reason why the Earth exists, for the diversion of the mind, for the mind to get involved with or confused by the material world. Amongst this confusion, some people find the real thing, and they have enough patience within themselves to not run around from one worldly thing to the next. They can just sit. They can really be. They can stay put. That's why the Earth is here.

BABA: The key here is, "Then it means even more…. If enlightenment is just given to someone who hasn't…."

SHARAM: Good point Baba. If enlightenment is given to us without us really striving for it....

Existence is striving towards becoming absolutely free, so it can become mature. Growth is there only when you have an option to become enlightened or not. Then growth happens. Growth is very exciting and that excitement is the reason that Existence happened in the form that it did. This beautiful place is given to us: nice trees, oxygen, prana, water, waterfalls, lakes, beautiful clouds, rain, snow, beautiful birds singing. So much is given so we can grow, and when we grow, Existence grows. Only for growth, do we come to duality on Earth: male and female, night and day. It easily can confuse us, but among that confusion we grow and our growth means more joy for Existence and more joy for us as a part of Existence.

THE TABLE

SHARAM: *(Talking about a student)* Her sitting was about the table. They bought a table *(chuckling)*. You guys know—"the" dining table. *(Laughter. Most of us have heard the story before.)*

The story: *A group of Sharam's students were all living in the same house. They decided to buy a dining room table for the house and asked Sharam if he would help them pick one out.*

SHARAM: They really insisted that I should go with them to buy this table, and I did. There were many, many tables there. I said, "Well, let's get this one, it's only one hundred and twenty-five dollars," *(chuckling)* but they chose one that was one thousand two hundred fifty or somewhere around there. I told them, "That's not practical, get this one." They insisted that "No, no that one is cheap; it's no good." So they bought the one they wanted over what I chose for them.

Since they got this table, it's been giving them so much trouble, so many problems, one after the other. The last thing that happened was Farin was cleaning underneath this table. She got up and her nose hit on the edge of the table and was bleeding and almost broken. Fortunately it didn't break, but when her nose hit, it made a big noise and blood was pouring everywhere. I have been telling them for years that the table was bad news and that they needed to get rid of it. Finally, they agreed with me.

(This table has created more problems for this group than is imaginable, much of it involving money, related to who should pay for the table and how much each person should pay. There have been many arguments and much discord in relation to it, so when Sharam talks about bad juju, he isn't exaggerating.)

SHARAM: Now they're taking it to the dump. The only thing is, even by taking it out to the dump, it probably will give them some trouble or another. You know what the dump will be, it's eight bucks. Still they have to pay some money. Who's going to pay for it now? *(chuckling)*

Anyhow, the point is, if you have trust in the teacher, which means you believe that there is a certain connection with Existence through this person, if you ask them something, and then you do the opposite of what they say, deep inside you feel guilty. You feel, "Why did I even ask?" And then this guilt ... usually when you feel guilty, somewhere along the way you hurt yourself. Somewhere along the way, the subconscious or the unconscious will fight with the consciousness. It goes against the table, for example, and the result will be some negativity that you create around you. That big negativity will cause some negativity outside and your nose breaks down and bleeds, or you fall down with the bicycle when you're going with the dictionary.

Who doesn't know about the dictionary story?

The Dictionary Story

Leila was working on her English skills and needed a dictionary. Her husband had lent one to Sharam, so Leila came to ask if she could have it back. In asking, she was very harsh and demanding. Sharam had several dictionaries, so he didn't care about the dictionary—it was Leila's energy that was the problem. He didn't say anything at the time, but as Leila was riding her bike home with the dictionary, she was very nearly hit by a car at an intersection. She was knocked over, the car missing her head by inches. The dictionary, however, wasn't so lucky. It was run over and destroyed.

Sharam described this incident in the same way as the table above. Leila was rude to someone she respects. Sharam wasn't concerned about her rudeness, but she was, and the war that began between her conscious and subconscious, as a result of her rudeness, caused enough negativity to create the incident with the car on the way home.

READY TO BE WHATEVER YOU WANT ME TO BE

The next two sittings happened as one, but again have been divided for subject matter. Jesse is describing her previous sitting with Sharam where she was talking about other people being jealous and selfish towards her.

SHARAM: There is no such a thing as jealousy and selfishness. Doesn't exist.

BABA: Only the ego has jealousy and selfishness and it's....

SHARAM: No

(He claps, standing up and rubbing his hands together with glee.)

SHARAM: Let's make this a play. Who wants to play?

(laughter from all)

RABIA: I will.

SHARAM: Come on and play. *(He motions for Rabia to stand up and come stand beside him in front of the class. They stand right next to each other.)*

SHARAM: Alright, I'm standing and she's standing with me. Look at her face. Look at my face. Everyone, just look at our faces.

(Light laughter from the room. Rabia seems a little embarrassed to be in front of everyone, but she is smiling and very happy. Sharam has a big smile on his face. There is a long pause as everyone is looking at their faces.)

SHARAM: Do we have ego right now, do we have any selfishness? Does she feel jealous? Do I feel jealous? We don't! I don't have any jealousy towards her, and she doesn't have jealousy towards me. But watch what will happen right now.

(Lots of laughter as Sharam walks around and stands in front of Rabia and tries to look somewhat stern. There is a long pause while we all watch him and wait. Suddenly, he cracks up and starts laughing before he says anything. Everybody laughs with him.)

SHARAM: What do you get from this? What am I trying to do? What's going to happen? I am going to be commenting, or doing something.... She's not saying anything. I will be saying something to pull out her jealousy or pull out her selfishness. I will say something and she will become very selfish. I also can say something so that she becomes very loving. She's just standing there. *(He points to Rabia still standing there.)* It's all up to me. I can make her jealous, or ... I can say something very kind, she will become very loving. It has nothing to do with her.

From her perspective, she can do the same thing. She can create jealousy in me, or selfishness, or she can create love in me. Okay? But let's say she says something that creates jealousy or anger or whatever in me. Then I have two choices. I can be kind to her and she will automatically become kind or, if I am just an idiot, if I'm just someone who doesn't have any understanding at all, then I go and stand in front of her ready to be anything she wants me to be. I am at a loss. She has the control. I'm just there, and if she says the smallest negative thing, I fly off the handle. I'm ready to be angry and blaming and to say to hell with her. I'm not in control. Anyone who thinks other people have jealousy or others are selfish is simply missing some understanding. Any of you who think like that are very immature! Someone who's mature never ever thinks that other people have selfishness or jealousy. *(Rabia tries to sneak back to her seat and everyone laughs.)*

SHARAM: No, stand here. *(He motions to her previous standing spot.)* I'm telling you please, wise up! Don't give in to your ego! And don't feel bad if you do. The ego is always ready to feel bad. Always, always, always is ready to feel bad. Please, have substance. Don't fall into other's game. If Rabia has the freedom to make me jealous, or to make me feel selfish, I have the freedom to do the same thing to her. It, most of the time, starts with us. You know why it starts with me? Because first, I think she's selfish. It starts with me. If she thinks I'm selfish, it starts with her. If I think that she is very nice, I'm wise. If I think she is selfish, I am a child. Really a child! I haven't grown. If I think she's selfish, it is because I am the one who allows it.

At what point am I mature? When I never see anything negative in anyone. That's the maturity point—the moment when I never, ever, ever, ever think that Rabia, or any of you, are selfish or jealous. If I see jealousy in you, I am at fault, not you. If I see you being selfish, it only shows something about me. Only me, because I am too immature, and I keep inviting her to put me down, by being immature. If you're mature, you don't invite anyone to put you down. Nobody does.

(Motioning to Jesse now) Look at her face. *(Talking to Jesse)* Since you've been sitting here today, you've been inviting everyone to not like you. Look at you: your face is inviting it because you are not centered. You act like you hate everyone. You invite people not to like you.

Now, what is the mature way for her to be? To understand that it's all her. It has nothing to do with anyone else. No one has permission, if I don't give them space. No one has permission to put me down, to be jealous of me, or to be selfish with me. No one! No one! No one! No one! It's all about me, not about anybody else. *(pause)* In a sense, you are mad at yourself. You're mad at yourself, but you project it, the mind projects it, onto others. *They* are selfish. In reality, I am just mad at myself, because I am just a child, because I haven't grown. But I project it. It's all Mona's fault. No, its Jerry's fault. No, no, no, it's Baba's fault, Debby's fault. It's Melina's fault. That's what the mind does.

So, I'm standing next to Rabia. *(He moves over and stands next to Rabia again. He is smiling, she is giggling.)* What am I doing? I can create a space where she will be very jealous and she will act nasty to me, or I can create a loving space. It's all about me.

OH YES YOU DO NEED IT!

Sometimes when Jesse is upset with others or feels they are picking on her, she says, "I don't need this."

SHARAM: Lower quality shouldn't overcome the higher quality. If you say *(speaking loudly)*, "I don't need this negativity!" That's the wrong thing to say. Whatever happens, you need; otherwise Existence wouldn't make it happen. So when you say, "I don't need this…." that's not part of the reality of Existence. That's only the ego talking, saying, "I don't need this hassle." ***Oh yes you do need it!*** That's why it happened. Someone who says "I don't need this" is very far from Existence. If we don't deserve something, Existence wouldn't allow it to happen to us. This is true for both negative and positive things. For example, "I don't deserve this hassle," which is negative; or "I don't deserve all this love," which is positive. Both are fallacies. Both are false. If we did not deserve it, it would not happen. But if we say, "I deserve it," this also will lead to ego gratification. Let's say I decide to pay for a holiday for you and you say or think, "I deserve this. I worked hard for this." That's ego gratification. *(pause)* There is a higher order or higher law and our mind, which is a juvenile, will not understand that higher law. This higher law is that everything that happens, God wills it, and if the mind says, "I don't deserve this," the mind is a baby. Very childish.

When God allows something to happen, how can we say we don't deserve it? It is just because we cannot see the wisdom of this thing in the moment that we think we don't deserve whatever is happening or we reject what is happening. Believe me, you need it for your growth, otherwise it wouldn't have happened.

JESSE: What about free will then? For example what does it mean if I can change something that is happening?

SHARAM: Then change it! *(Chuckling)* Do it! Then that thing becomes what God is willing at that moment, if you change it. *(Pause)* If you change it, then Existence is changing it. Everything that happens, Existence is happening.

(To Jesse) When someone does or says something you don't like you often say, "I don't have to take this!" Don't say, "I don't have to take this." What I mean is that those things are happening and we should look at them. This is part of maturity—that we don't question things that are happening. *(Chuckling)* Instead pay attention to how you respond to things that are happening. If you question, you are questioning God. If you have problems with what is happening, you have problems with God. If you criticize what is happening, you are criticizing God, or Existence.

*"A mystic takes care of things very gently.
For example,
'Thank you for pulling on the grass like that,
so I can remember to tell the others
not to do that.'"*

–Sharam

BYPASS THE EGO WITH SUBTLETY

JESSE: How can we tell someone that they're doing something wrong without picking on them?

SHARAM: You have to bypass other people's egos with subtlety. *(pause)* Okay, let's say you pick on me. You can only pick on me if you bring negativity. If you're positive, you don't pick on me. You can tell people whatever you want with subtlety and you're not picking on them, you're not saying negative things. If I say to someone, "Hey why did you do that, shape up! Why did you do this negative thing?" then I'm picking on her, but if I say, "You know if we can do this differently, that would be really wonderful. What you're doing is great, but there is a different way of doing it too. Let's look at that one too, compare the two of them, learn something." You see, we can say anything we want with subtlety and things will change.

TOOL KITS

ANN: Why hasn't my passive/aggressiveness changed?

SHARAM: Everybody has one negative thing. It is the means or the focus of their growth. Yours is being passive/aggressive. So passive/aggressiveness has to stay with you forever, just short of enlightenment. If you let passive and aggressiveness go, if you pass that stage, you will never become enlightened. It is your aid, your tool kit. You need to have that. It is something that was built into you for this lifetime, to help you.

ANN: Last night while I was in the middle of negativity, you were telling me to watch my ego. I could see what was going on, but was powerless to do anything about it.

SHARAM: The powerlessness to do anything about it is the best approach. If you had power to do something about it, then the ego is doing something about the ego, which would be garbage upon garbage. When you are powerless to do something about it, that means the ego is stepping aside and you are letting it go.

If you could watch it, fine. If you could not watch it, fine. Existence is doing its job the best for you. If you can't watch it, then the issue persists. It is necessary for it to persist. It is cleansing more. I am just giving you a dose of trusting Existence one hundred percent. Everything that happens has a much higher reason that the mind doesn't get. It comes from deeper than the mind.

ANN: When I fall into this, it feels like a nervous breakdown. I can't talk, I shake.

SHARAM: When you shake, it means you have gone deeper into the issue, which has been condensed so much. The issue that gets so compressed becomes like petrified muck. So you are hitting this muck that has been petrified for so many lifetimes. Of course it gets harder. So, yes, you shake, but then we work on it, you get a deeper understanding, acceptance comes, and you get out of it.

ANN: I still condemn myself when I fall into this negativity.

SHARAM: Condemnation is a very interesting thing. It is fascinating. More and more, we see, as we go along, that the only reason that we fall apart is because of condemnation. Condemnation is amazing. All the time, growing up people tell you how bad you are. Either directly or in subtle way they say, "You are worthless," or "You need to be different," or "What you do is wrong." They condemn you, so now you condemn yourself.

Condemnation throws you into hell and then you get delivered from hell to heaven. Every time you come to heaven, you come higher into heaven. Every time you fall into hell, you go deeper into hell, getting to that petrified stuff. You see, we have to come out of it and jump back into it again, come out and jump in. We are here to cleanse it. You have to do it. You haven't done it for thousands of years. To heck with that. You are going deep and cleansing. Be happy.

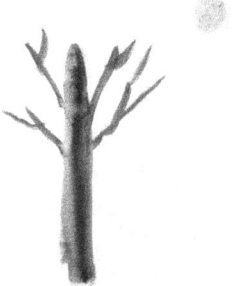

BECOMING ONE WITH NEGATIVITY

STREAM: My son is visiting from New York this weekend and yesterday, he, Sean *(another son)* and I went out "boondocking." We wanted to use the Jeep and Sean took care to be sure it was in good shape for us. He even rotated the tires. Well, when we got up to 50-55 mph it started shaking so bad that we couldn't drive it. We had to go back and get my CRV. Sean was really, really angry about the situation. You could just feel the rage. And it happened a second time during the trip when he thought he had lost his cell phone.

It makes me really uncomfortable when he gets that way. It makes everyone around him on edge: his brother, me, and I don't know what to do. I want to make him feel okay; I want to make him able to handle things. I don't know where his anger comes from and why he goes there.

SHARAM: We want to be total. We want to become one with Existence. Existence means what? It means positive, negative, transformative. We want to be one with Existence, but we hate negativity. We can't become one with the negativity. Isn't that interesting? If something goes negative, we hate it. But that is also Existence, and we want to become one with Existence, one with God…, but we hate that part of God so passionately. How can you become one with something that you hate? You can't. That's very simple.

Negativity is part of Existence. If you accept it, you stay in it for a minute, maybe 3 minutes. If you don't accept it, you will get stuck in it for a long time, maybe a lifetime, maybe a few lifetimes.

This applies to anyone: Isn't it interesting? Your son doesn't accept the fact that the car has some problems—for God's sake, it's just a car. Sometimes, they break down.

And then, your son losing things, losing his cell phone. These are the times that Existence goes to negativity. What we should do is just look for the phone without anger or being upset, and if we don't find it, we simply buy another one.

STREAM: So do you think this is stuff that I can talk to Sean about? I don't think that he would understand any of it.

SHARAM: No, you have done the damage. You taught him. In the past, when something went wrong, you got angry in front of him, and he learned that negativity is bad. So it's a learned behavior. By becoming conditioned, by learning, we separate ourselves from God, from Existence. We learn that negativity is horrible. So we separate ourselves and then we suffer.

STREAM: And even my discomfort with his negativity is confirming that negativity is bad.

SHARAM: Yes. What you should do is, if he gets negative, you should enjoy it as much as you enjoy the positivity. That's the best thing. You can't do anything for him, but you can do something for you, which gradually will transfer back to him. Very gradually, because, before, when your son or anyone was a baby or a small child, the mind was fresh. There was nothing in it. At that point, you implanted in him that negativity is bad. Now, as an adult, the mind has so much stuff in it that things have to go gradually to change. It will take time.

So in an indirect way you can make a difference. The funny thing is that you get upset at his negativity, but you expect him not to get upset by some negativity! *(Laughter)* We don't apply it ourselves. "No, you should not get upset! But, if I get upset it's okay...."

If you grasp this deeply and apply it, I call you an enlightened person! When something goes negative, that's part of Existence and it's as great as when something is positive. When we look at things this way, what do we get? A happy person all the time: happy, happy, happy. That's all we need to know. Long story short, in a nutshell. The whole Existence in a nutshell. Maybe not even a nutshell, a pistachio shell.

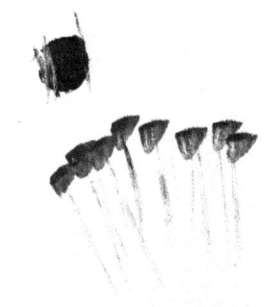

GAINING MATURITY?

This sitting occurred a few days before Livia's brother and sister were due to arrive from Germany for a four week visit. She is concerned about the length of the visit and feels that the problems are already starting before they have even arrived.

LIVIA: I see that I bring out all the bad things in other people that aggravate me. Right?

SHARAM: Yes.

LIVIA: That sucks! I can't come and complain about them.

SHARAM: Are you becoming mature? *(Smiles)* Come and complain. Just know that this is a play *(interacting with others and complaining)* and you have to do it.

LIVIA: As long as I realize that it is really me bringing that out in them, I can manage. If I can stay centered, I can always say, "That was me." As you said, be more subtle and have more understanding, but I don't know if I can always do that. I would have to meditate five hours a day to get there.

SHARAM: I have a meditation for you that would really help you. Smile to your heart. That will really make your whole day smile.

SITTINGS

LIVIA: I won't be able to come as often while my brother and sister are here. When do you think I should come?

SHARAM: You enjoy the sittings, so come for those.

LIVIA: When are the sittings now?

SHARAM: My understanding is that I come and sit here, and if there is a need to talk, we do the talk, because meditation and openings, both are really meditation. The point of meditation is to bring you to acceptance. The point of sittings is to bring you to acceptance. They have the same goal. I feel that if there is any issue, we better do that over the meditation. Meditation you might be able to do by yourself, but openings happen when we are together. If I am here, my priority for now is, if there is an issue, we will talk about it.

THE PATH OF LOVE AND THE PATH OF MEDITATION

CHRIS: Since these five months of exercises are finished, I have become really lazy. *(Chris and others in the group took on a five-month commitment to meditate and do breathing exercises for two and a half hours every day.)* I work on the book or meditate when I want to. I know I'm on the path of meditation. Should I set up a more disciplined schedule?

SHARAM: No. Your path is changing. Your connection with me is getting stronger. Your feeling of love for me is becoming stronger. Gradually, you are coming out of the meditation path and coming to the path of love. On the path of love, you are flexible. You are not so attached to a schedule. That is why you mentioned that you are lazy now. The meditations have made you more female and the laziness that you feel is you feeling the female side which you have been conditioned to believe is laziness.

EXISTENCE IS SO LAZY!

*Rain falls out of the sky
From clouds unwilling to carry its weight,
Hitting the ground with a pop
And a splatter,
Puddling in the low spots
Then flowing downhill,
Riding on the coat tails of the Earth,
To the Ocean.*

CEMENT

ANN: I see that I am comparing myself to Sophie and her work with her parents. When I think about going back to visit my family, I see that I am not ready yet, but she dealt with hers so beautifully. I see that I have changed, but not nearly enough to deal with that yet.

SHARAM: Sophie was fifteen and a half years old when she came to me, and this is eleven years now that she has been working on herself. She was only fifteen and a half, so she had become less cemented. When you came to me, you were forty-five years old. You have more cement to break.

RESISTANCE

ANN: What does resistance mean?

SHARAM: Resistance means fighting with God. Resistance means running away from the higher self. Resistance means thinking that you are very important, maybe the most important thing on Earth and nothing else matters. It is very selfish. Resistance means not taking responsibility. It means running away. Basically, the biggest tool of the ego is resistance. We all resist, and, if we don't, we will be enlightened. Our resistance can be very subtle or very gross. There are many different levels of resistance.

ANN: Why do I resist so much? Why do others not resist?

SHARAM: We have to expect some resistance here and there. Your background is different from everyone else. Everybody has their own unique path to get to the top of the hill, the mountain. I had better call it a mountain because the ego wouldn't like it if I say hill. You have your own unique way and sometimes you need to resist. Inside you know when to resist and when not to. Your soul knows what is best for your path in this moment. Don't compare your resistance with other people. Just watch. You used to resist every minute, all the time. See how much you have grown. If you say, "Why does she never resist and I do?" that is where we fall into difficulty. It is actually a big demand on God. You are asking, "Why is her path that way and mine this way?" She probably worked on herself in past lifetimes, let's say ten thousand years, while you worked on yourself only nine thousand. She worked one thousand more years than you, so she is more like water, while you have to resist a little bit longer. It is okay. It was your decision. You said, "I want to stick with the world, get drunk all the time and have fun," while she was working on herself. It was all your decision in the past lifetimes. Now you are doing really good. If, in this lifetime, you all become enlightened, who cares if you started a thousand years later or earlier?

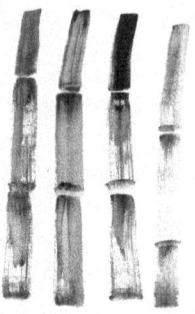

REPEATING HIMSELF

SHARAM: When you are in the mind, the mental body, or in the emotions, the emotional body, or in the physical body, or in *any* body, I have to repeat something over and over and over and over for it to go totally to your soul. It is not only the emotional body—it is all the bodies, unless you are in your soul. Then I do not need to say anything at all. We sit here. I close my eyes. You close your eyes. We don't need to say anything. The purpose of repetition is for it to go deeper in you. You noticed it because of the book. You don't want to repeat things over and over in the book, but when I share it here, it makes sense. When you want to write it down, it is a little bit different.

I repeat something many times because the objective is not for it to become a book, but for you to get it deeper inside your heart. If there is something that is repeated many times, it is being looked at from a different angle. I know when something goes deep inside of you and when it doesn't. When it doesn't, I repeat.

Buddha has said we have to repeat something one thousand times before it hits home.

THE MACHINE VS. THE MOMENT

Sharam started this session by saying, "This morning is for meditation, but one person can talk if they need to." There were some mixed messages in that the schedule said meditation, but we had talked earlier about the meeting being for sittings. One person came up and talked, but Ann was upset at not having a chance to share, so Sharam called her up too.

ANN: I thought this morning was for talking, not just meditation.

SHARAM: All talks are petty. All talks are nonsense. For example, in the old days, when you entered a temple, they told you that you could talk once a year, only once, and only one sentence, so you stay there for a whole year to talk only one sentence. I don't do that. I am not tough and hard like that.

ANN: I was a mess last night. Do I hold it in until our designated talk time? How do I work through this? Do I express right away, or wait and let it get worse like I am today?

SHARAM: There is a reality on Earth. People fall apart, they get messed up, and somehow they deal with it. They work with themselves. If you always think that I have to quickly be there any time you fall apart and solve it for you. I become your crutch.

ANN: How do I work through things when I am a mess, and not use you as a crutch?

SHARAM: Understand that you are a perfectionist. You have to be perfect. You have to be better than everyone, and now you think you should not use me as a crutch. Don't be a perfectionist. Today was planned as a sitting, so we have to have a sitting or you fall apart. Everything has to happen according to what is planned. You have to be the best. If someone is better than you, you fall apart.

Everything *is* perfect, just as it is.

You say, "I shouldn't be here" because you aren't perfect. "I have to be perfect." Just now, the reason you fell apart was because, in your mind, you weren't perfect. Now, because of that, you are suffering. The Earth is not a place for perfection. Allow imperfections. Be happy with them.

ANN: I still don't know what to do to work through my issues.

SHARAM: Again, because you have this view of perfectionism, you don't want to do anything wrong and you are worried that coming to talk to me outside of your sitting time is wrong. Life is not so dry, so black and white. It is more colorful, easier.

This is why you are being healed, because I am not like you. You are very tough and inflexible. You cannot allow for any spontaneity.

Now, because of what I just said, you will think your life ends, and that you had better leave because again there is something that you are not perfect at.

The world has told you that perfection means everything is in order, but here we keep changing the rules on you. Perfection is not that. To be perfect means to be flexible. It is hard for this to go in because of the cement that they made in your head for years and years and years. You are like a machine. The programming is very deep-rooted. To change this machine takes years. You are a machine. All I want is for you to be a free spirit, like a free soul that can fly and be happy, but you are so rigid. Society told you this is perfection, that everything has to be on time, according to plan. Changing your plan in the last minute, they've told you, is bad.

ANN: The reason I was counting on the sitting this morning is because I was such a mess last night, but now you say all talking is petty. I'm just trying to figure this out.

SHARAM: Again, this is structure. Anything I say, you stick to that. I contradict myself later, but you stick to that one thing. Do you see how structured you are?

Figuring out means focusing on all the dumb structures. Don't figure out anything. They taught you always to try to figure out things with what you have in the mind. *(quoting Ann)* "When you came, you said that all talking is petty, and I'm trying to figure it out." This is so structured. I've said ten thousand other things to free your soul, many in this sitting, but you stick to this one thing. Do you see how structured you are? Structured. Structured. Structured. Structured. Structured. I keep repeating it.

ANN: Last night, or any time you are tired, I don't want to ask you anything.

SHARAM: Give me the freedom to tell you I am tired. Don't assume that I am tired. This is passivity, when you assume that this person is tired. Just say, "Sharam, there is something that is heavy on my heart and, if you are not tired, can I share it now, or should I wait until tomorrow?" At least then, in the morning when I come here to sit, I know that you have something to say. I wouldn't walk in here and say that no one should talk and we will do meditation. But you don't give me that chance. You sit down with this whole world of structure and perfectionism in your mind and with that, you create a reality for yourself based on something I have said in the past, and leave the rest of us in the dark. You are so passive. Then, when too much pressure comes, you jump in and say, "I have to talk." You go to aggressive. What happens in between? There is a quantum leap from total passivity to total aggression.

ANN: I am sorry.

SHARAM: Let's talk about you being sorry. Being sorry means that something wrong has happened, and I am sorry. Nothing wrong happens. Everything is perfect. Even when you say you are sorry it is perfect, but know why you are saying it. Everything is perfect. We just have to know why we are doing it. I'm sloppy. Sloppiness is perfect. Why am I doing it?

Ann, as usual, your sittings got the best out of me.

THE MACHINE

News
Hitting the printing presses of
The mind,
A roller coaster of recycled moments
Manipulated and headlined
Slapped onto recycled paper
Cut and compartmentalized
Fluffed and folded.
In Arabic or French
English or German
Yesterday's or breaking
All old
News.
Repeated over and over again,
In that sticky Web of the ego…
The mind,
The ultimate mechanical millipede
Stepping one thousand times
Over the same ground
Endlessly trying to catch up to
Now.

ANY MOMENT

ANN: You said I would remain passive/aggressive until I reached enlightenment. You said this is a tool that I use to work on my issues. Do I want to get rid of it?

SHARAM: Of course you want to get rid of it, because you want to get enlightened. You hold on to this until you get enlightened, but of course you want to get rid of it. You don't need to carry this forever. At any moment you can become enlightened. Don't think that in ten years and twenty minutes I will become enlightened, so I have to carry this until then. At any moment, you can become enlightened. Any moment! So of course you want to get rid of it. It is going to be your tool, but at any moment you can become enlightened and throw that tool away. It's like your car. When you need to go somewhere, you get in your car, but once you have arrived at your destination, you don't take your car in with you. The tool has to be thrown away.

ANN: It feels like I have so much to do.

SHARAM: That is why you have so much to do, because you feel like you have so much to do. Whatever we feel, we carry with us. In ten years you will think, "I have so much to do." Because you are thinking it now, you will think it then. Throw that away. With enlightenment, you never know. *(To Livia, who is often worried about paperwork she is not getting done and the messiness of her house.)* Never carry the idea that you have to get through all your papers or work. Maybe while you are still going through your papers, you get enlightened, because we said the messiness is perfect too. Everything is great. If you want to clean your mess, that is perfect too. Just go through life remembering that everything that happens is perfect. It is just the way Existence wants it. Everything. Every single thing.

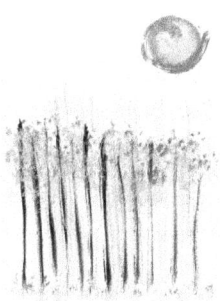

PATHWAYS TO THE EMOTIONAL BODY

SHARAM: I talked to Scott and Barbara on the phone in a sitting. Barbara asked me how come a woman falls into the emotional body, and how does it work? And then Scott said, "Why do I forget everything, but she remembers what I said a year ago, and she complains constantly about it? I don't even remember what I said a week ago. How come it is like that?"

I talked about the movement of energy. That is because the man mostly sticks to the left side of the brain, in the male side. His energy is focused there, and there's no pathway from the left side of the brain to the emotional body. You can only go from the female side of the brain, the right side, to the emotional body. Most women stick to the right side of the brain. Now, the energy moves around in a woman and goes to a certain memory in the female side of the brain. All the emotional issues around that memory are sitting inside the emotional body. So when she has a memory, the energy pours down the pathway from the right side of the brain to the emotional body, and all those emotions get activated. Then she becomes emotional about something that happened two years ago, ten years ago, a day ago. But the male doesn't have that avenue. You have to go to the female side of the brain.

So in the male side, the energy goes to a certain memory. It remembers and then the energy moves on to another memory. The energy goes so fast that sometimes you don't even remember the memories, because the energy doesn't stop anywhere. The only reason it stops in the female side of the brain is because it drops from there into the emotional body, so you stay with that memory for a long time while you are dealing with the emotional body.

This is the way it is. This is how you cleanse your emotional body. You are a woman; you cleanse your emotional body. And then, after you clean it, you don't have anything in there. Then the next lifetime, you become a man—because you don't have anything in the emotional body to cleanse. So, now you are a man not doing anything with your emotional body anymore.

In the old religions, they used to say that only men become enlightened. Buddha did not even want any women in his religion, because he said it's a waste of time. "I can do nothing for them. They have to die and become a man; and then they come back and come to me. And then I help them out." And many religions didn't even want women, because as long as you have so much blockage in the emotional body, they couldn't do anything, they couldn't—*really*—they couldn't help. Because they (the religions and their teachers) were not subtle enough. Today we can, I can. I can help. *(Laughter because all the people in this sitting are women.)* Thanks to twenty-five hundred years passing and the understanding that has come in that time.... I've been so many times a woman and have so much dealt with my emotional body, that I understand it and I can help with that.

DEBBY: How about a man who drops to his emotional body?

SHARAM: Okay, the man will fall into the emotional body only when he switches to the female side, which sometimes happens. Most men are always thinking. Because they are mostly thinking, a lot of energy doesn't switch to the female side. A little bit of energy goes to the female side, a lot of it stays on the male side because they have all this thinking to do. But sometimes, when something emotional outside happens, like their father dies or something, then they fall into the emotional body. With you, nothing emotional outside needs to happen, just a memory, and you will fall into that emotional body. With a man it doesn't work that way. If they watch a very emotional movie, for example, then the energy slips into the female side, and goes down to the emotional body. Mostly the stimuli have to come from the outside for a man, for that to happen. Thank you. Good question.

POVERTY OF THE MIND

LEILA: Anytime I don't have money, I fall apart. Does that come from my mind or does it come from a chakra?

SHARAM: If you have money, you feel more self-confidence—you have more self-confidence—you get things done, but if you don't have any money, you feel poor and you lose your self-confidence. But poverty is not about having or not having. Poverty is an issue of the mind.

There is a poverty of the mind. There is also a material poverty. It is part of the growth of human beings. Every human being should have this material poverty. This belief that I don't have enough. There is a scarcity, you see, there is not a diamond in the world for every single person on earth. Really there is not enough, even water, for all these people to have. We really have to be careful with that. There is a scarcity. And this scarcity causes scarcity in the mind.

But money also relates to the first chakra. Overall, if the first chakra is open before certain maturities of other chakras are reached, if it is premature, it is dangerous because the first chakra is also the source of our kundalini energy and this energy is extremely powerful. If there is a blockage somewhere in our chakras and it hasn't had much work done on it, releasing the powerful energy of kundalini all at once, can cause an unbearable amount of cleansing which leads to insanity.

On the path of mysticism, a mystic works on all the other chakras at the same time that they are working on the first, so that when the first chakra does open, this very strong kundalini energy can easily clean what is left in the other chakras. This is why the seeker will have financial issues all along until they become enlightened. Opening the first chakra fully will be one of the last things they do. Existence makes sure that money or security issues are implanted in us by parents or society for our own protection.

For example, my mother and father never really focused on any financial or money issues. So I never worried about money. However, when I was sixteen or fifteen, somebody said, "Sharam, will you lend me some money?" and I did. He said, "Next week I will give it back to you."

So the next week I said, "You owe me money, will you give it back?"

He said "I'm not giving any money to you. Forget it."

He was so happy to steal my money. That was the first time I was confronted with somebody taking something from me. I thought he was so irresponsible. I had never encountered that before. It was just WOW, I couldn't believe it. So I never forgot that. My mother and my father never really had any money issue, but I had that experience with a friend.

(To Leila) Money means security, so if you feel like you don't have that security, right away you fall into the first chakra. But remember, your worrying really makes things worse.

The First Chakra

SIGNS OF AN IMBALANCED FIRST CHAKRA: Fear, feeling insecure, sorrow, depression, numbness, not trusting, not having self-confidence, being greedy, physical problems like sciatica, being too fat or thin, constipation, hemorrhoids, prostate problems, varicose veins, lower back pain, addiction to food, alcohol, or sex.

SIGNS OF A BALANCED FIRST CHAKRA: Feeling secure, not having fear of people, centeredness, feeling peaceful, good relationships with others, being accepted by others, trusting others, most of the things we do make us happy and satisfied.

THINGS TO DO TO MAKE THE FIRST CHAKRA STRONGER: Walking, biking, running, yoga, gardening and sitting on the grass.

EGO AS DESIRE

SHARAM: Let's look at three parts of the ego: the mind, the emotions and desire. Desire relates to the movement of energy. Desiring is the result of our energy, our kundalini, not moving. When our energy isn't moving, we feel stuck or incomplete, unhappy, and desire arises. The mind and emotions merge to implement desiring. We get emotionally involved with our desires and we use the mind to figure out how to achieve them. If we get the object of our desire, or do something that we have been desiring to do, we are happy. The mind is conditioned that if we get what we want, we are happy. Why? Because mind, which is really the ego, needs to be higher than others, and if desire comes, or that thought comes and we don't implement it, the ego falls apart. It feels inadequate, or not good enough.

The desire could be, if I get a new car it makes me happy, or a better job, or if I meditate, it makes me happy. If I awaken my kundalini, it makes me happy. Any desire. If our kundalini moves, we won't have a desire; if it doesn't move then we have desire—and that's ego.

I have never looked at ego from this angle before. It is a new definition for me. When you're totally exuberant, when you're radiating light, and you're absolutely content, there's so much energy moving, in the moment, in you, that there is no ego.

But remember, until we become enlightened, we have ego. So to condemn desire, to say it is bad or to try to stop it doesn't help our growth. We have to understand it more and more, to see how much everything we do—almost everything we do, or think, or want—all comes from the ego. Don't condemn, just understand and watch.

THE BEST SITTING OF RABIA'S LIFE

Sharam mentioned to Rabia that she had said or done something to someone that had bothered them, had created an issue for them. Rabia reacted by becoming negative and condemning herself.

SHARAM: Never, ever say anything negative about yourself. The only reason your face is teary is because you're thinking negative. You can do this. It just takes time. You can't become a doctor overnight. You can't become an engineer overnight. You can do this, it just takes practice. It happens gradually. This is a brand new thing for you, not putting yourself down and not thinking negative things about yourself. They couldn't build Rome overnight, but they built it. You can do it.

You won't be hurt if you don't think negatively about yourself. If you don't put yourself down, if you don't say you hate yourself, you won't be hurt. You will not say, "I'm hurting" anymore. I promise you. You won't even cry. You'll be very happy, if you don't think negative of yourself, if you catch yourself. Gradually, but surely, it will happen. It's big work not to put yourself down. Your problem is simple. You always put yourself down. It's much better than putting other people down because you can do something about it. Work at it. Write it down, very big, in a notebook: "All I have to do is: Not put myself down and don't think negative things about myself."

RABIA: I can't express myself or speak.

SHARAM: You don't need to express yourself. There are many paths. Your path is to not put yourself down. It is not about expression. If you want to become a master, then you need to express yourself. An enlightened person doesn't need to express anything, nothing. Only a master does and you're not going to be a master, you're going to be an enlightened being. As a matter of fact, enlightened beings don't express anything. They are just silent. Meher Baba became enlightened, and for years he was silent. He just looked at the wall for years. Then Existence wanted him to become a master, so he had to express and even then he wouldn't talk. He would write things down on a board. He never talked. He didn't break his silence. You never know.

RABIA: Why can't I just accept that I'm not cut out for this? Not good enough....

SHARAM: Don't put yourself down. Every time you get emotional and cry there is something negative that you're thinking. You're putting yourself down. Put it into positive terms.

RABIA: What's wrong with me? Why can't I just accept that I'm not up to this? I'm comparing myself to people who are better than I am and I don't want to accept that I'm worse.

SHARAM: It's not about better or worse because there is no better or worse. Use some other word please, because you're getting somewhere. Don't go to illusion. Good and bad, better and worse are just illusions. Get to something more concrete please. So who is better than you?

RABIA: Everyone who understands. Everyone who can express themselves. Everyone who is more mature.

SHARAM: Because you are more silent, you are much higher than them. Do you know what they express? They express that they are falling apart, a mess. They express their problems. Someone who doesn't express on this path, they are either repressing or they are more advanced, and I see that you are more advanced in this area. You just compare and you put yourself down. That's all Rabia.

RABIA: Okay. I'm going to listen to what you've said, and I'm not going to talk about it anymore, other than not putting myself down. I'm not going to talk about anything else. I'm getting off the track which I've been famous for in the past.

SHARAM: You just put yourself down. What you did just now is a temper tantrum. What you're telling me is, "How dare you say a negative thing about me? If you say anything negative about me, I'm going to raise hell around here."

See you say negative things about yourself. It's only a front, it's only because you want to hurt others. Really, what it is, is, "How dare anyone put me down! How dare you tell me what I should do or not do!" It is revenge. You don't let anyone put you down. The slightest negativity or criticism from me and you are going to raise hell by putting yourself down, because you know, when you do this, other people get really hurt.

RABIA: I'm sorry. I feel very bad.

SHARAM: Feeling sorry is again the ego tricking. You're really good. Your ego feels really good. So anytime anyone says the smallest criticism of you, you are going to punish them deeply. Understand that you manipulate people, you want to hurt them. You don't want anyone to criticize you or tell you what you did wrong. You don't want to hear it. In a very subtle way, you let them have it. Not directly, because you think you can't, you're not powerful enough. They will be stronger than you if you directly fight with them. So you do it very sneakily, by putting yourself down and they get hurt.

RABIA: I hate this. It's disgusting. I don't know how to make a positive out of this.

SHARAM: If you say I hate this, you're doing it again. If you go to negativity about this, you're doing the same game. If you don't go to negativity, people don't get hurt. You will have a good time too. It will be a win, win situation. Right now, your ego says I don't care if I lose, as long as I get them.

RABIA: I don't want to ever forget this. I don't want to slip back into this.

SHARAM: It's good you taped this—the most important thing in your life, ever. This is the ultimate, the deepest issue of Rabia. This is the deepest, deepest issue. I'm glad you have understood this so well. The smallest thing, if somebody criticizes you. For example, I told you that you said something that caused an issue for someone, and you started crying and you put yourself down. You said, "I'm not cut out for this, I want to leave." You know that you are not leaving, and I know that too. You just want to hurt.

Everything the ego does is to hurt the other person because the ego says, "How dare you tell me that I did something wrong! I'm going to get you in the worst possible way." Your ego is very sneaky. It doesn't attack me, it attacks you, which is supposed to hurt me a lot. It hurts anyone who is talking to you. It works perfect to put yourself down and cry. The other person gets so hurt and they can't do anything, they get paralyzed. If you attack them, they would attack back with a vengeance. But you are putting yourself down. They hate it, they suffer, and your ego enjoys it immensely. The ego stands there and says, "Ha, ha, ha, screw you! You can't do anything, you're paralyzed. How dare you criticize me?!" It is so amazing. There is nothing the other person can do. They hate it, they hate you. They don't even understand how they fell into this trap.

RABIA: I never understood this before. I never understood how I did this before. I'm afraid I could fall into this again.

SHARAM: No, I don't think so. You've understood this very clearly. I think you can catch yourself. You understood this so well.

RABIA: I'm not sure I understood it so well. But you explained it very well. *(laughter)*

DOUBT: TAKING A FEW STEPS BACK TO LEAP FORWARD

SHAHED: My question is, I'm not sure if I'm in rebellion or what's going on for me, but I feel like it has been going on for months. I'm not eating well and I don't meditate. I don't have trust or faith in healing. You've tried many times to tell me to try this or do this to stop a headache or heal myself, but I don't have faith in it. So, I'm not sure what's going on. This morning I was thinking, my life is so lackluster on the outside and yet I still don't have this passion for enlightenment and I've just been kind of feeling, "ugh, what the heck?" So that is my question. *(smiles)*

SHARAM: What I hear about the passion, you don't have a passion for enlightenment, the only way to get the enlightenment is to drop the passion. So I see that as something very positive. When you say that you lost your faith or you are in doubt, I see this as going back a few steps to jump even further. We've been doing that all the time with you, Shahed. Now it is less, but before was every couple of weeks, twice a month I think. That was really good, to not trust and then jump to a higher state. So what I see is you are preparing to do a jump. Now maybe the jump is right now, maybe tomorrow, but these are the symptoms of going back to jump forward. It has been like this from the beginning. With other people this happens more or less, but with you it has been a source of your growth. It has gone deep in you throughout the years that you go back, then jump forward, back and jump forward. All that to me is a good sign.

About healing. There is no such thing as healing. Everybody is whole. If somebody brings some karma around a place in the body, they create some karma and I clean that; I don't call that healing. Healing doesn't exist. Karma exists and then the karma is cleaned. I don't believe in healing. I believe in someone wanting to do something so strongly that they do it, or they don't do it. It's just about whether their subconscious wants it or not. This reminds me of the doctor who was charging a lot of money for anything that he did and he had nearly one hundred percent success. Another doctor, a better doctor than the first, charged very little. He had only fifty/fifty success in operations, healings, whatever. Just because the first doctor charged more, people believed he was better, so the people who really wanted to get well went to him, paid a lot and got well. It's just about what we want or don't want.

SHAHED: But you believe in ... well ... you don't believe in anything....

SHARAM: I *know* that there is karma because I see it. You have to believe in it. To believe means to doubt. Belief means half doubt and half wanting to accept. Like this camera, I don't need to believe in it. It is there. I see it.

The karma is there, I see it. Then one day it is not there. I see that too. Then I see that the depth, the totality of the person wanted it to go away, so it went away. I see that the karma listens to your totality. I see it.

SHAHED: Yes, *you* see it which is great.

SHARAM: And if you doubt it, that is great also.

SHAHED: I don't see it! I don't ever feel that totality. That wanting it so much. I might feel total for a few moments with you ... I heard what you said that not wanting enlightenment is important, but I see that the people who are really working on themselves are really moving along.

SHARAM: So you see that. You see that they are moving along. You tell me that you don't see anything.

SHAHED: Well I see it in them.

SHARAM: Good! That's how it's supposed to be. They see it in you. You see it in them. They don't see it in themselves. Ask anyone here. They don't see it in themselves, but you see it in them. The reason for this is, if you see your growth, your ego takes credit for it and you stop working on yourself, because you think you're so wonderful. Existence is so perfect.

SPIRITUAL ROOT CANAL

There was a situation where a misunderstanding happened between Ann and two other students. Ann felt ignored and excluded by them. Even though they did acknowledge her presence, she still thought they could have done more to include her. Her ego, like all of ours, is always on the lookout for actions of others that support its beliefs—in this case, that she is not wanted.

ANN: It is back to the situation in the back room again with Roxana and Rabia, and the sitting that followed. In the sitting that followed, I had a lot of resistance. I didn't want to hear anything. Listening to the tape, I still go back to that same place, even though we've talked about it since then and worked on it. It still carries me back there.

SHARAM: Which is good. If it wouldn't carry you back there, then we would have to wait for another situation like that to happen. This is very good that you go back there, so we can work on something concrete that has happened. We would have to wait another few months or even a year for that thing to happen, so I am so glad you go back there.

Because the issue is not resolved totally, it is like there is decay in the tooth. In a root canal, they make a hole below the tooth and they want to get the pulp out. The doctor gets a long metal instrument, like a small knife. He goes in a little bit, and pulls the stuff out. He goes in a little bit more, and pulls out. Then, they fix the tooth. You go home, after a week it starts hurting, you go to the doctor. He says he has to go in and get more out, because we missed some. Then, they finally get the bottom part and it is all out. Every two minutes they get an x-ray to see how much more they need to get, and sometimes, it doesn't even show.

This is the same thing. We keep digging and cleaning the roots, getting the pulp out of this issue. You understand part of it. You feel good because you understood something. We don't go further. We wait until you go and listen to the tape again. You come up to fresh pulp that has to be pulled out, and we work on it in the next sitting. If you don't go back there now, I'm sure that in a few months, it will start hurting again. This is exactly the process and procedure that we do here. I am the dentist.

Still some roots are left, and we have to do the pulp cleaning.

ANN: Why don't I want to take responsibility for my part in what happens? It seems the only way to get it is to take responsibility.

SHARAM: Because usually that is what happens when we get a wound—we don't want to take responsibility. This is a characteristic of that decay. But gradually, we clean it and you get a little bit more responsibility. Like today, you are a little bit more responsible than before. Even noticing you aren't taking responsibility, that is taking responsibility. Before you would just swear at your mom and cry and think everyone is wrong. Today you are talking about why you aren't taking responsibility, which means you want to take responsibility. That is a big step. Many of those roots have been cleaned. You feel less hurt and because there is less pain, you understand better.

"LOVE ACTUALLY"

Love actually is all around us
In the air we breathe
The snow that falls
The breeze,
So
Breathe it in,
Roll in it,
Throw a ball of it at a friend,
And
Laugh as it drips inside their collar
And down their back
Pay attention as it caresses your cheek.
Fill yourself with it
And, then,
Relax
Let go,
Someone will catch you
If not,
There's always the snow.

FEELING INCLUDED

CHRIS: I have such a problem with not feeling included. What is the best way for me to look at it?

SHARAM: Just remember what we said today. Everyone has that wound. If somebody doesn't include them, they don't like to be there, and if they are welcomed, then they love to be there. In you, it is a bit deeper wound, and we are working on it. Because of this deep issue, you have always stayed on the fringe, not at the center, with your friends and relatives. Others have this issue, but not so much. Therefore, someone like Torry or Debby, they are at the center of their family and their friends, because this has not been a deep issue for them. They have more self-confidence in this area. You are gradually getting there.

If sometimes things become tough, it is only so some wounds can come to the surface and get cleansed. Everything is pure love. We mess everything up, and Existence helps us to clean it.

WE ARE NOT HERE TO LIVE, WE ARE HERE TO GROW

Rabia was upset: she thought someone was acting horribly.

SHARAM: We are not here to live. We are here to grow. Living hasn't worked very well so far!

RABIA: So, it doesn't matter how I feel? Or what they did to hurt me? Should I just pretend that everything is okay?

SHARAM: No, not pretend. Have some compassion for them. Be compassionate. Be loving. They have had a lot of problems. You came to me some years ago. We were at an event downtown. You saw the people and you said, "Thank you Sharam. I'm so glad my life isn't this anymore!" It's time Rabia. Please do something for yourself. Watch yourself, notice if you're excluding someone. This person is really helping you to grow.

*"Nothing in Existence is wasted.
If someone is nasty to you,
it gives you an opportunity
to not get upset,
and them an opportunity
to look at their nastiness.
It's all about growth."*

–Sharam

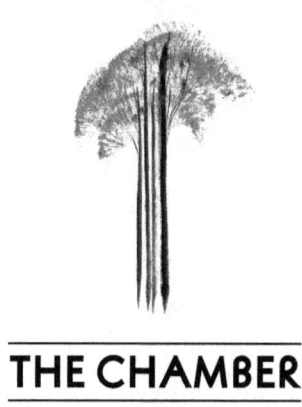

THE CHAMBER

Livia asked Sharam if she could see him in private to talk about an issue she had.

SHARAM: You are very smart.

LIVIA: I am?

SHARAM: Do you remember what you asked me the other day when Torry and I walked around the pool?

LIVIA: Yes, if I could walk around the pool with you as well, on our next group sitting. You said, yes. Thinking about it though, I would prefer to sit with you in your chamber instead of going around the pool.

SHARAM: Chamber? *(The group discussed the meaning of chamber: judge's chamber, torture chamber, gas chamber.)*

SHARAM: You take advantage of every situation. My remark of being smart was sarcastic. Your mind thought it was a compliment, but your subconscious knew it was a put-down and responded with the word "chamber," a negative way of describing my room. You were defending yourself subconsciously.

LIVIA: That is greedy. My god, I am so greedy!

SHARAM: I am glad you can see that.

LIVIA: How do I defend myself subconsciously?

SHARAM: How does anybody defend themselves? By trying to say that the other person is wrong. We don't see our part. We say, "I don't have an issue," that's how. All that comes from the subconscious. It is very subtle. Sometimes we don't even see the other person doing it *(defending)*. When we don't see it in others *(With the "chamber" comment, the group immediately reacted to the word, but didn't catch on that Livia was defending)*, we feel a little bit icky, but we don't know why. People just feel that they don't like you.

LIVIA: Just when we have an interaction, or also any other time?

SHARAM: Any time. Many people do feel it, they are more in tune and more subtle, they see what's wrong with you. But there are millions that don't and they just feel yucky. That has changed in you though; it is much better now. Before you were not subtle at all, but today you are much, much better.

LIVIA: Is there anything that I can watch?

SHARAM: No. You will watch only to the extent of your capacity. All you have to do is expand your capacity to become more subtle. Then you will see it. As your consciousness expands, it can see the more subtle stuff in you. Let's say this white piece of paper is your unconscious and it is about eight inches wide and eleven inches tall and your consciousness is this small *(the size of a quarter)*. As your conscious grows, you see more of the white paper. So the more subtle you become, the more your consciousness grows and you will see the parts of your unconscious that you couldn't see before.

LIVIA: Next is the question of me taking advantage of every situation, that I hook into other people's issues to clarify that subject for me. Is that taking advantage or is it a good thing?

(Often, after Sharam has talked to another student about an issue they have, i.e. anger, Livia will then ask about her anger level. Or he may suggest breathing to a certain chakra for cleansing and afterwards, Livia will ask what chakra she should breathe to. This is what she means by "hook" here. She is asking Sharam if she is being greedy by doing this.)

SHARAM: If it helps you it is a good thing, if it helps the ego, it's a bad thing. Every situation is different. So, when you have a question, just ask me, "Is this coming from my ego, or is it for my growth?"

FACELESS BEAUTY

A cat burglar broke into my fortress
And with velvet voice and faceless beauty
That scoundrel picked the locks
Of my most sacred wounds
And stole my heart.

DESIRING

GOD'S BIGGEST FAN

People say, Buddha too,
That all desires are
Food for the ego,
But I prefer to look at things differently.
Master says,
"All desires are a desire for God
And the way to God is meditation."
So the way I figure it,
I'm God's biggest fan!
Cause right now
All I can think about
Is getting out of town
To water and sunsets
Where the wine runs freely
As does the gourmet coffee
And the food, Ahh!
Sweet corn and pies

> *Potato salads and pork chops,*
> *And bread slathered in butter.*
> *Mm, mm, mm!*
> *The question is*
> *How do you resist that kind of longing*
> *While convincing yourself to sit*
> *And seek this abstract notion of God instead?*
> *So I'd like to propose a new motto:*
> *"All meditation leads to pork chops and pie!"*

SHAHED: You said in your reading that if we don't have desires, anger, jealousy, sexuality, we don't have....

SHARAM: Sexuality, anger—most of these come from desire. If you don't have desire you won't get angry, you won't become sexual, you won't feel jealous. So really, really we've got to focus on that desiring. That's why Buddha focused on desiring. "Desire *not* with all your heart," that's what Buddha says. Just desiring.

SHAHED: And that *(not desiring)* comes from meditation, awareness?

SHARAM: Both. If you meditate, your consciousness, your awareness, your witnessing grows. You can catch yourself while you are desiring. It only takes one catching. If you catch yourself, it's a done deal. And then, focus on desiring. You have homework: for a week, anytime you're desiring, catch yourself and write it down. Maybe you will catch yourself only two times. Better than none. Then get another week from me to watch your desiring. You might catch yourself three times or one time. Just watch for those desirings and write them down. Very soon you will see that, in the fifth week, you've caught yourself ten times desiring, halleluiah! And then very soon, six months passes and you catch yourself all the time desiring. Then I say, "Congratulations, you are not losing any energy," and you will notice that you are not getting mad. You are not worried. You won't be jealous. You won't compare. You won't put people down. The ego is calm.

TWO BIRDS

SHAHED: I notice that my mind is always beating up on myself or it's beating up on someone else. How does the ego benefit from this?

SHARAM: Let me relate it. When you beat on someone else in your mind, you are beating people up; that's very clear, your ego likes it. The ego loves it because the ego feels, "Wow, I'm better than Rabia," for example. The ego loves it. Now, why do you beat on yourself? When you feel that you are not better than Rabia, that comparison, "Rabia did that so well, she did this thing.... Oh my God, I never can do it the way she does it." With this comparison, you start beating on yourself because your ego seperates itself from this Shahed that isn't good enough. It says, "How dare you not be better than Rabia?! You thought you were better, now you are not. You see, Rabia can do this and you can't do it. What the heck is wrong with you? Get up there and do it better." *(Laughter)* So now it's like Shahed is another person.

When you are on the path, or if you have been on the path in past lifetimes, you will hear over and over that you are the consciousness; don't get identified with the outside, or with your name, or with your face or your thoughts. These are not you. Then your ego uses that in a very subtle way to separate itself from you and to beat you up by saying, "You are not good enough," and all you feel is, "Oh my God, I am not good enough."

People who have never heard about mysticism and things like that, they don't hit themselves. Someone else is at fault. Like Denise. She never blames herself. "Only other people are messed up. I'm the best." No matter what, she doesn't put herself down.

DEBBY: When you say, "I am the worst," you are feeding the ego also, right?

SHARAM: When you say you are the worst, because the ego is beating up on yourself, it is feeding the ego.

SHAHED: Who is the person that's watching this going on and is uncomfortable with it?

SHARAM: If it is uncomfortable, it is the ego. If it is comfortable it is the self, the consciousness. Nothing can disturb the consciousness. It is the ultimate watcher. It's like one bird sitting on top of a tree, watching two birds fighting on the lower branches, jumping from this branch to that branch and this branch. That one bird is your consciousness. It sits there all the time at peace. So inside you there are three birds.

SHAHED: So what is it when I start beating up on someone else in my mind and then there's the voice that comes in and says, "Hey, what are you doing?"

SHARAM: Right there that outside person is gone, and now there is only you and you. Before, there was you and him, or you and her. There is no more an outer person, But as soon as that outside person comes back in, you again become united against them.

FARIN: So Sharam, are these two fighting birds inside of us fighting over good and bad, our beliefs about what is good and what is bad?

SHARAM: It could be good and bad. You can look at it that way. The whole thing originates from that. Hell starts from good and bad. These two birds are the ego and sometimes they become one and fight against another or they become part of you fighting another part of you.

SHAHED: So jeepers, I'm witnessing a little bit because I see myself attacking someone on the outside, but then, I immediately lose it and start fighting with myself. So … what….

SHARAM: That's why when Denise or others have a conflict with me, after I leave, they start fighting with themselves and they say, "Why did you do this? This is horrible. He's your teacher. You need him. He has helped you…," and then they come and apologize. When the inner dialogue happens, they start beating themselves up and they want to apologize and correct it.

SHAHED: So with all this fight, we are still leaking a lot of energy.

SHARAM: Like crazy.

SHAHED: What I see is that I'm fighting all the time in my mind and that all my energy is staying in the mind.

SHARAM: Okay, Nima asked a good question. He asked, "Sometimes we have too much energy and we have to throw it out. What is that? You keep saying that we need to collect all this energy, but sometimes we have to throw it out."

I said, "Well that's a very good question. You have a few layers. You have the body, which has energy; you have the mind, which has energy; you have the heart, which has energy; and you have the soul which has energy. When we start desiring or getting angry, because anger and desiring are very subtle, we lose energy from the heart or the soul. You start leaking from there, but we do not want to lose energy from the heart or the soul. The only energy we need to lose is from the mind.

The mind becomes mind intensive—it's disgusting. But soul intensive is great. That's where enlightenment comes. Ecstasy comes."

SHAHED: How do we lose our energy from the mind?

SHARAM: To lose energy from the mind, you have to bring the energy from the mind to the body with deep breathing, sleeping, taking a shower, a cold shower, sex, shouting, or doing an active meditation (shaking, shouting, or hitting pillows).

SHAHED: I am thinking that we must have a boat load of energy the way I throw it out all the time.

SHARAM: We get more energy because we breathe. When you breathe, you bring in a boat load of energy. Thanks God that you are breathing.

THE MATHEMATICS OF LOVE

SHAHED: Sometimes I feel love so intensely, like for you, during the day let's say, and I feel like I have to get on the phone and tell you, *I Love You!* Like I have to get it out of me. So last night I said to myself, okay, it's okay we don't have to say anything, let's just feel this love. Let's just have it for ourself, and the love energy stayed inside and I felt a lot of healing happen.

SHARAM: When you intensely feel love, Existence takes that energy where it needs it for healing.

SHAHED: So is it good to hold it in then? I am wondering what is that rush to get it out of me for?

SHARAM: That is beautiful. If you hold it, it heals. If you share it, more love comes to you. That's the mathematics of it.

SHAHED: So just one more question then. I see that, in terms of sharing love and stuff, I feel that my mind is very negative, and that I have to really force it to think positively. It even struggles to share love. Are all minds like this or what creates such a negatively focused mind?

SHARAM: Mind, because for years and years and years of the energy going around and round and round about the same things over and over and over again, the mind gets stale. It gets bored and the boredom turns sour, turns to negativity. So the mind always wants to pull you towards negativity because it is bored. It isn't having fun. If you give lots of breaks to the mind, it feels happier; but right now, the mind constantly works, so it gets tired. When you are tired you become cranky. The mind is cranky too, so it is negative. But the mind that you give lots of oxygen to by deep breathing, meditation and silence, loves you, will produce the best things for you, will go to positivity for you. You sensed what I was saying right now.

SHAHED: Yes, I know exactly what you are talking about, but my mind went to criticizing myself for not being more meditative.

SHARAM: Don't. Go to the positivity. Tomorrow you will do it. Every day, I get up and I say, "Today I will lose weight," and then I see at night that I haven't, but every morning I say, "Today I will do it," and it never happens. Which is good. I'm so glad I am positive. *(lots of laughter)*

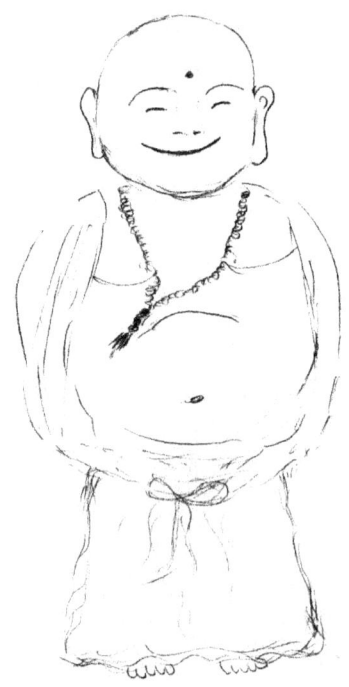

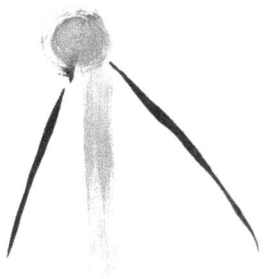

THE THREE STEPS OUT OF PASSIVITY

Stream started her sitting by describing the inner excitement she felt while she sat waiting for Sharam to come out. She was excited because she felt she had something interesting to share. Then her mind turned to worrying, saying, "Well, maybe it's not so good after all." Finally, after worrying for a bit, she went to Sharam and let him know that she was getting antsy and wanted to share in the group sitting before she had to go back to work, thus breaking her passivity.

SHARAM: Do you see the steps? Three steps. There are always three steps to being passive/aggressive. The first step is when you're passive. You sit there and worry, but you don't do anything about it. The second step is when you are not passive anymore. You worry about something, but eventually you do something about it; but, because you are worried, there can be the element of aggression in this step. You aggressively do something about it. The third step is that there's nothing to worry about. You just sit there and are happy. If something needs to be done, you get it done, but assertively, not with aggression.

STREAM: Take what comes.

SHARAM: You don't even take it. You just go with whatever comes. Don't take it, because even taking is an effort. You just are open. You

(Stream) are on the second step. The first step and the third step look alike, but there is a big difference! With both you sit there, but with the first one you are boiling inside. With the third one you are in a let go. They look alike on the outside.

Stream described the influences from her childhood on her personality which produced passivity in her.

SHARAM: When you were passive, you had it all. You just had to let go to be on the third step. You could have jumped past the second step. The second step is very hard to pass. You guys think the first one is difficult; try passing the second, to go to the third. It's really difficult to jump from when you aggressively want to get what you desire, to becoming assertive. Passive, aggressive, assertive.

So, you don't know how good you had it when you were simply passive *(on the first step)*. Sometimes you were outwardly happy with it, but, in the back of your mind you were always thinking, "Maybe this passivity is not good."

STREAM: Well, that was imposed on me really heavily by my husband—the idea that my passivity was not good and that there ought to be something more to me than a pretty face.

SHARAM: If there is assertiveness it is great. Not in the form of passivity, not in the form of aggression, but in the form of a let-go, it is great. Today you were trying to come out and express yourself. You said to me, "I'm getting antsy." But why? Why would you want to get antsy? Because it's a group sitting and you feel you should talk? Just sit there and relax in your meditation. Whatever happens, happens. Silence is higher than talking, so if there is silence that's great. If there are noises everywhere, that's also great, because you can be silent among the noises. That's an even higher silence because your silence is not conditional. Anything is great; just go with that.

I AM BETTER

"Anytime I get hurt it is because I think I am better than everyone else."

Sharam had been gone for several days and had just returned. When he got home he rushed to the bathroom and then was talking to another student. Ann was hurt and it was obvious from her face that she was not happy. She felt she was being ignored. She hid and when later confronted by Sharam, said that she didn't want to be in the way.

SHARAM: The ego is fooling us. How? *(to Ann)* You think that the reason you hide is because "they" don't care. They don't need me. I am in their way. I am not good enough. This is the mind. The ego, behind the mind, is saying "I am more important. I will show them." The ego gets hurt because it thinks it is the best. It gets hurt and says, "How dare they do this to me? I am mad at them." It is the ego saying it is the most important. The mind says, "No, I am not important," but the ego has a different agenda. It is more subtle than even the mind. The mind has been around for maybe thirty, forty, fifty years. But the ego has been around for thousands and thousands of years.

The mind is millions of cells, all of which are empty when you are born. Then you start filling it by putting memories in it. These memories could be something you read, or some experience you had, or a fight you had, or a talk you had, or a TV program you watched. All the cells get filled in this one lifetime. The ego, however, is in a deeper part of your mind, carried over for thousands of years. It is very subtle. The mind cannot be that subtle. The ego uses the mind for its purposes. The ego is saying, "I am better than other people." The mind says, "They don't care about me. I am not important. I am hurt." So, anytime I get hurt, it is because I think I am better than others. You get hurt because you thought that somebody didn't care about you, but deep inside, you behave this way, you withdraw, because you think you are better, because "who do they think they are? I am better than them and they are ignoring me."

ANN: How do you get past all this ego that is so deep in there and so strong?

SHARAM: The only way to pass it is to consult with me. Your ego is no mystery to me. It is a mystery to you. What you do ninety-nine percent of the time is that you fight with everyone, including me, in favor of the ego. Consult with me. I know the ego in and out, from every angle. Don't defend so much. Remember to come and ask, "Is this my ego? Am I being egoistic?" Anytime you are hurt, it is because you think you are better than everyone else. That means the ego is at work—every time. When you get hurt, instead of escaping and hiding, come and say, "I am hurt. What can we do about it?" When I feel something is important, everything else has to wait. So take a chance. Tell me you are hurt, ask me if you are being egoistic. Maybe this is very important.

*"If we don't ask for what we need, we suffer.
Then we make those around us suffer too.
If we ask for what we need, it is done.
We don't mess up the space
and disturb others,
so ask for what you need.
Don't be selfish."*

–Sharam

EXPECTATIONS

ANN: Right now, I'm noticing a lot of twitching in my left eye. What is going on?

SHARAM: This eye twitching relates to stress, stress that arises from one of your biggest issues: the idea that when someone has said we will do something, we should do it as planned. If it is within the schedule, the plan, then we have to do it as planned. How destructive it is. How we lose. It creates twitching in our eyes. It creates expectation and expectation destroys our growth so much. Your sittings, for example, they have to be on time. We can't meet on another day or you fall apart. How much this destroys humanity.

ANN: You said to come forward at every group sitting and try to chip away a little bit more at what is going on.

SHARAM: Just because we said it before, you are doing it. Let's see how that is destructive.

ANN: Should I let it go, then, and not chip away?

SHARAM: If you let it go, then it is another destruction. So what to do? If you come and try to chip away at it, from the angle of expectation....

You see, because I said something, there is an expectation in you to do it. That is where the destruction is. If it is just something that happens spontaneously, in the moment, then it is very constructive. That is what we have to understand. There is a fine line between spontaneity and saying, "We said we should do it this way, so we should do it because we said it." The second is destructive. It really pushes us into the dark hole, because of the expectation behind it.

ANN: One of the things you have been telling me lately is to ask you, and then to listen to and follow what you say. You have been saying that I ignore what you say. If you tell me something *(come up every sitting)*, how can I be spontaneous and yet follow through with what you want me to do?

SHARAM: There is a fine line between these two. You have to find that fine line for yourself. Before I tell you exactly what it is, which I already did say, I already said it a minute ago....

You said something very beautiful. You said you had a sitting, and that you listened to a recording of it once and it became more clear. You listened to it a second time, it was better. The third time was good, the fourth time was wow, the fifth time was, "Oh God. Now it dawns on me what Sharam was saying. Now I get it. The fifth time, transformation dawned on me. It was great."

I already gave you the answer just a minute ago. It didn't sink in. You need to listen to that recording. Also, you need to find that fine line between not being attached to what has been said, or promised, and the spontaneity of the moment.

ANN: Can you tell me what you said a few minutes ago, or is it better if I listen?

SHARAM: I will say it again. I'm going to say something new. If we remember what promise has been given to us and we want it to be delivered to us because it has been planned, it has been said, it has been promised, a deep expectation arises in us. Expectation is like poison, poison for our soul. There is a lot of "not understanding" in it like, for example, every day is a different story, a different stage in our growth, and every different stage has different requirements. Different things are necessary. Yesterday something else was necessary. Today, a one hundred eighty-degree opposite thing is happening, but if we apply the same understandings or "plans" from yesterday to today, we are ruined. We are not allowing for this difference when we say, "You promised this yesterday. Why is it not happening? We scheduled this. It has to go according to our schedule." There is a fine line between being spontaneous and going with expectation. That fine line is that, with demanding, there is not deep understanding. With spontaneity, with here and now, there is a deep understanding. Making a schedule and following it is very helpful in day to day life, but sometimes going with the flow in the moment is what our being needs, more than what we have scheduled. So, anytime you say, "Listen, this was planned…." know well that the ego is at work. Understanding is missing. Anytime.

NEGATIVITY AND EGO

JEANNETTE: I've been thinking a lot about negativity. Last Wednesday, you read about it and I was noticing that I have been negative a lot. Even when I'd wake up in the morning, I'd have negative thoughts. So that Wednesday night, I told myself to be positive or not to think negative thoughts, and ever since then, I've been thinking positive thoughts. Even in the morning I have positive thoughts. During the day, I'm not depressed as much as usual. I'm not sad, and I'm feeling so much more positive towards myself than I have in the past few weeks.

SHARAM: This is great. Sounds good.

JEANNETTE: So how does one go into something like negativity?

SHARAM: We don't do it, it happens. Something outside will trigger us, a thought or a feeling will do it, which are all from the outside.

JEANNETTE: How do you work with it?

SHARAM: Now we know that you fall into anger or negativity from outside. The question is, when you fall into negativity, how do you work with it? It depends if you are on the path of love or the path of meditation. If you're on the path of love, which you are, what you do is bring understanding in. With the path of meditation, they have to sit there and meditate.

JERRY: So when anything happens, your conditionings tell you to react in a certain way. If instead, you just stop and say, "Wait a minute. Is there another reason this could be happening?" And then allow for another reason....

SHARAM: Perfect. You are breaking your conditionings right there. Every time you break your conditionings, you go to acceptance. If you don't accept something, it is because of your conditioning. Even our reaction to the phrase "F--- you" is a conditioning. If you spoke Chinese, you wouldn't know what is "F--- you." So you see, even that word is conditioning. Aggression, however, is the same everywhere. If you are in China or Egypt or anywhere, when someone is angry, it is the same. Everyone understands anger. Anger is a universal language. Love is a universal language. So what to do with anger? With anger, you just say to yourself, "Break the conditioning. My conditioning is that if somebody gets angry with me, I should be angry back at them, but that is crazy! I don't want to follow that. Right now this person, *(say your husband)* is angry, but in two minutes he will not be." If he was an angry man all his life, then, you have married an angry man. Then, there's something wrong with you for marrying this man in the first place and you need to look at that.

JEANNETTE: Basically it's all about acceptance again.

SHARAM: Yeah, it's all about that. Letting go takes us to acceptance, understanding. This morning, I was saying that a lot of people have acceptance, not total acceptance, but to some extent, ten percent acceptance, twenty percent, five percent, some people have fifty percent—different ranges.

JEANNETTE: Different times, too, because we are not all accepting all the time.

SHARAM: Right. Today, you are accepting; tomorrow, you might not be accepting of the same thing.

JERRY: It's like before, when you said if anything bothers you, it's your ego.

SHARAM: Yes, it's the ego.

JERRY: That bothered me, when you said that. It feels right, but it's still hard to accept in certain circumstances. For example, getting cut off in the car by someone; it immediately bothers me.

SHARAM: And what is the ego? The ego is our interpretations, our conditionings. In this case, the conditioning is that if somebody pulls in front of you, you get mad. What is understanding? Well, I did the same thing myself many times before, so it is okay. That's understanding; that's accepting. Understanding brings acceptance.

JERRY: The other thing you said about the ego is that it thinks it is more important than everybody else: you shouldn't pull in front of me because I'm better than you.

SHARAM: Right. Now, if you think someone is better than you, like the President of the United States, if he is driving and he pulls in front of you, because you think he is better than you, it is okay.

JERRY: Or if it is your boss, and you don't want to get fired, so it is okay, too. Although with my boss, I still wouldn't like it. My ego would still be bruised a little.

SHARAM: Only because you think you are better than the boss, but if you truly believe the boss is better than you, then the ego steps aside.

JERRY: So if the ego really believes somebody else is better than me, then I won't get upset.

SHARAM: Right.

JERRY: But anybody we don't know is automatically not as good as we are.

SHARAM: Right. It is very rare for the ego to accept that somebody is better than him, very rare. It will be a big battle between the ego and the self. The ego really fights to make sure that nobody is better than it. That's why the slightest mistake of someone else is a big deal, but if you make a mistake, it is okay—just a mistake. It's okay for us, but not the other guy.

THE EGO IS ABSOLUTELY GREAT!

Sharam had just commented on a change in the level of anger in another student during a group sitting.

LIVIA: Can I ask you about my anger level? Is this an ego question now or is it a question that helps me grow?

SHARAM: All questions are ego-based. Ego is there for you to grow, so ego questions are there to help you grow. If it were not necessary for you to grow, the ego wouldn't be there. So, let it be written:

The ego is absolutely great!

That snake that talked to Adam was the ego and wow, it is helping Adam so much. I see that you hate ego. Please don't hate it; it is serving you so well.

About your anger Livia, sure I see anger.

LIVIA: Lots of it, right?

SHARAM: No, no. You are constantly cleansing your anger with deeper understanding. So you don't need to yell or hit the pillow. You have found a better way, which is deep understanding!

As soon as we become aware of our ego, most of us immediately begin to condemn it. But knowing that the ego is great and absolutely necessary for our growth, helps us to look at ourselves with openness and acceptance, with curiosity instead of condemnation.

THE BEAUTY OF BOTHERING PEOPLE AND BEING BOTHERED

SHARAM: If a problem goes on and on, that means you are growing. If it bothers others, it helps them to grow because it forces them to look at themselves. Always. Write it on a big piece of paper, "Bothering people is equal to helping them." Never stop helping them. Don't bother them on purpose, that is ego. Whatever you do that is bothering people, that is God helping them. If you go and pinch someone on purpose, that is not helping them, because the ego is doing it.

CHRIS: It is such stupid stuff that sends me down into negativity, and I can see it is stupid.

SHARAM: I am so glad it is stupid stuff. If someone dies, or you cut your hand off, or the house burns down, those are not stupid. I'm glad the things that bother you are stupid. That means you are lucky. If big things bother you, like your car blows up or this house burns down, those are big things. Small things? You are lucky. So lucky. Many people starve to death; big things bother them. You are so lucky. We have to get bothered to grow. So you see how much God loves you? You are so loved by God that big things don't happen. This is again another One Hundred Eighty-Degree Rule. Our mind doesn't know this. I am helping you to see it. You are so lucky.

RESPONSIBILITY REVISITED

THE WIND

Have you ever seen the wind
Time itself in a hundred meter sprint
Then go back to where it started
And do the sprint again?

SHAHED: I'm seeing a lot of things, but they still seem kind of vague to me. I don't feel clear about them. What does this mean?

SHARAM: It means you have a high expectation of yourself and whatever you see, you think this is not it, it's vague, not good enough—high expectation for yourself. I don't see any vagueness in you.

SHAHED: So the thing I'm noticing now is that I want to be sick because that gives me an excuse to not participate in life. With my husband, I tend to complain about not feeling well to somehow escape, and I even think my first chakra physical issue is for me a form of escape. I would prefer to start living and stop escaping. Can you help me with that? It feels like a responsibility thing, not taking responsibility for my life. Is that it?

SHARAM: The fact that you have a higher expectation for yourself, in a very subtle way, means that you don't want to be responsible for yourself. It means, "Look I am not good enough. I am not up there *(pointing to a place way above his head)* and it is really bad, it is horrible." It's really not taking responsibility in a sense. It's a good place to go and hide behind, this perfectionism, to avoid responsibility. And when you don't take responsibility, your body says, "Listen." In the chakra that you are stuck in, the chakra says, "Listen, she is not taking responsibility. Why should I?" It is giving up. The energy doesn't go there. If we don't take responsibility for ourselves, the chakras fall apart.

The first chakra in particular is getting worked on all the time. Basically the first chakra falls apart because every day-to-day thing we do, we operate from the first chakra. We go to the store, we say, "How much is this? Two dollars? Okay. I give you two dollars." Right there, when you are giving the two dollars, you're working on the first chakra. And how many dollars throughout the day do you have to pay? We buy this and that. So which chakra do you really work the most on? The first chakra. You always think about money. Don't waste electricity. Oh, I broke this. It costs five dollars. All the time, when money comes up, we are dealing with the first chakra. And if you don't want to take responsibility, by saying that I'm not good enough or by having high expectations for yourself, then the first chakra always has problems. It creates a problem in the body around that chakra. Why? Because any chakra you are in, if you don't take responsibility, you damage that chakra. So this is it, and then, also, if you are very controlling because of money, it also will come to the first chakra.

If we don't worry, if we don't have this high expectation for ourselves, we take responsibility and taking responsibility is fun. As a child, all of you have been pushed to take responsibility and you didn't want it. Now you don't like it. You hate it. You think it is bad, all of you, every single person. Taking responsibility is great. It's fun, but nobody told us that. For you taking responsibility reminds you of being forced to take the garbage out. You hear, "Take the garbage out!" You think that is responsibility. That is not. Taking responsibility is not taking the garbage out. It is not washing the dishes.

SHAHED: What is it?

SHARAM: Taking responsibility basically means to throw out that higher expectation you have for yourself. You always think, "I can't be good enough." Taking responsibility means knowing that you are good. That is what I was trying to tell Rabia. That she is wrong and wrong is right. That is taking responsibility. She is constantly afraid of doing wrong. You *(Shahed)* always think that you are not doing your best and that is not taking responsibility. Your best is what you are doing, right now. Whatever you do is your best and it is great. If you really incorporate that in your life, if you really apply it, if you really understand this, then you are free of this physical problem. You will be free of many problems.

SHAHED: Okay. I see that expectations are too high or that I create something I should be doing instead of just seeing who I am and liking that. So do I throw that expectation onto my husband then: "I can't do it, but you have to," or do I say he is judging me because I'm not good enough?

SHARAM: Both, you say both. You throw the responsibility onto anyone, and then you think they are judging you. As a matter of fact, thinking that someone is judging you is throwing the responsibility onto them. I think someone is judging me, what does that mean? It means that I am doing something wrong, which means, I should be better. There is a higher expectation there. That I am not this *(holding his hand up to the sky)* and that is why she is judging. If I am who I am and it is great that I am who I am, why would I worry about that judgment? Judgment? What is there to judge, this little spot on my shirt? What?

So if you worry about judgment, it means that you think you are not good enough.

SHAHED: Well, I'm thinking about the first and second chakras. That is where my body is falling apart. In a lot of ways my main relationship for not taking responsibility for myself is in my interaction with my husband, and then we have these issues with sex, where I am always resisting him, even when I don't want to resist him. Can you explain that?

SHARAM: It is really what you just said. It is about responsibility. You think this is something he wants. If he wants it, it is just like the father saying take the garbage out and you don't want to take it out. It is the same thing. It's you not wanting sex because he wants it. You have projected your father onto him. If he says, I don't want sex, then you say no, no, no, please let's have it. It's just that simple. It's just the memory of the father saying do something when you don't want to do it. Or it comes from the culture. You learn it in the culture. Even if it is not in your father. The culture goes inside of us. You gotta take the garbage out and if you don't do it….

With my mother it was the opposite. She always told me, "Don't touch the clothes, don't clean up after yourself. You're not going to fold the clothes." So when she was not there, I would fold the clothes and clean my room hidingly. When I heard her coming, I would throw all the folded clothes around and mess up the room, so she wouldn't get mad. Can you believe it?

SHAHED: So the other day, I had an awareness that the thing that really brings me joy in my life is looking at myself, gaining understanding. That's always been the thing that really fires me up and makes me feel connected. So I said, "Oh! That's what you like and that's what you are doing. That's what you love to do and that is what you are doing! Oh!"

SHARAM: That is wonderful. It's the first time in your life, because most of the time....

SHAHED: I am thinking that I need to be doing something else.

SHARAM: Yeah, you always thought you don't like what you are doing. I gotta do something else. So that's a big, big, big, big, big, very big step in your life. Congratulations.

SHAHED: Thank you. Thank you for helping me.

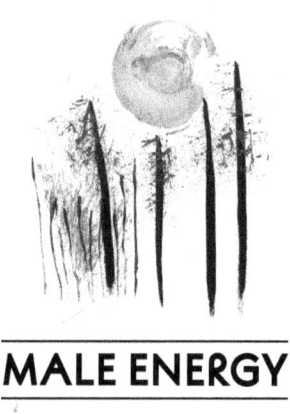

MALE ENERGY

LIVIA: Two days ago we talked about my being afraid of male energy stemming from my mom, who was more male. What do I do about that?

SHARAM: The reason Livia is afraid of male energy is because she has scary male energy herself. You are afraid of yourself.

LIVIA: If I thought it *(my male)* was that disgusting.... Even as a little girl, I never wanted to be like my mom, especially that part of her.

SHARAM: That's why you repressed your mother. The male side of your mother is repressed in you, and you are really afraid of it. If somebody is really tough, you hate it, because you hate your mother, and you hate your own repressed mother's male energy.

LIVIA: Is that why I explode every so often?

SHARAM: Sometimes, when you get pushed to the limits, the mother comes out and you hate it. You don't want to go there, but if you get there, you hate it. If somebody pushes you to the limit, you hate that, and if somebody else has that scary male energy, you hate that too.

LIVIA: I feel that it has gotten much, much better. I think I don't explode as often.

SHARAM: Are you repressing, or has it really been cleaned?

LIVIA: I think since you allowed me to be the bitch, it's gotten better.

SHARAM: I said for you to do it for a week?

LIVIA: No, you gave me free range, you didn't put a limit on it.

SHARAM: I am so glad you can be a bitch freely. I haven't seen the bitchy side in you recently. Maybe you forgot.

LIVIA: It really helped me when you gave me permission to be a bitch. Then I gave myself permission to just be who I am and freely express myself.

SHARAM: Is there anything about the sitting this morning that you hated?

LIVIA: I resent that our small group sitting has grown into the size it is this morning. *(Sharam had invited a couple to join us.)* I have watched it grow and was wondering if my growth has suffered because of it.

SHARAM: It is just the opposite. We become even more total by sharing in a bigger group. It helps you to really see yourself deeper and open deeper issues.

TRANSFORMATION MEANS ACCEPTANCE

SHARAM: Acceptance definitely brings you to the moment. Every time you accept something you are right here. That is what we call transformation. Acceptance is transformation. What if you are sitting there and there is nothing to accept? Can you be in the moment when there is nothing to accept? The mind goes through things that you are not aware of and are not accepting of, all the time. The mind is thinking, coming up with problems and ideas; it is not accepting, so you can't be in the moment. Sometimes you start smiling and are happy all of a sudden, because you just came to some acceptance in the subconscious without even knowing it.

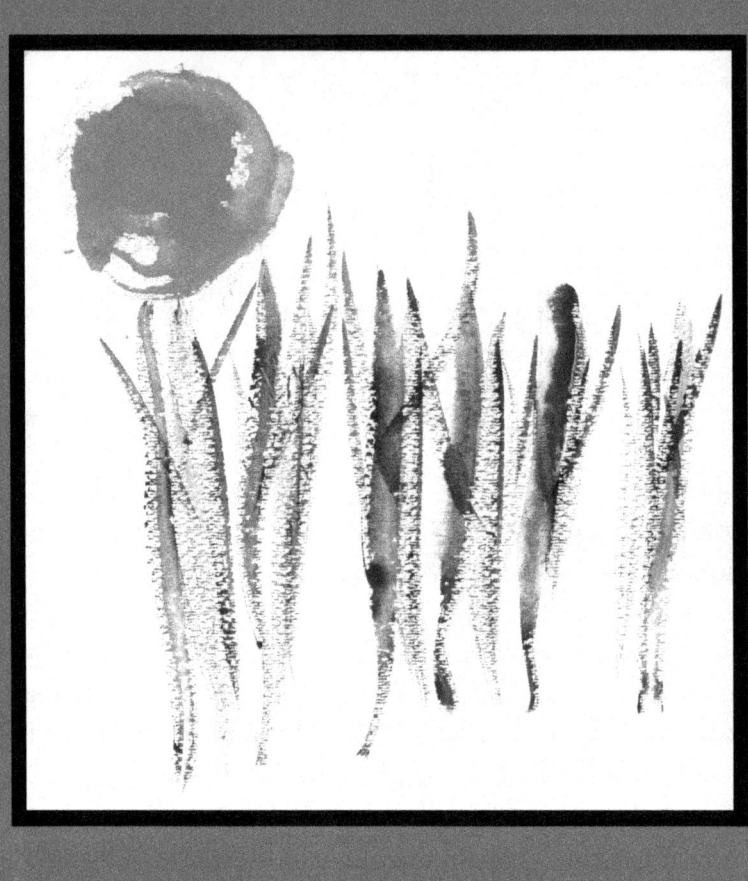

THE WAY OF THE MOMENT

Sharam was sharing some experiences he had on a road trip. The space became weak and he said the following:

SHARAM: When I share something that is fresh, something that is happening right now, the space becomes strong. Your heart opens up. When people tell stories, the space becomes weak. When we share something of the moment, all the hearts open up. Because the energy climbs all the way to the heart, the space becomes strong. Anything of the past or so much of the mind makes the space very weak. This reminds me of the movie with Jack Lemmon and Walter Matthau, *Out To Sea*. There was a guy who always talked about history. It was very interesting at the beginning, but it got boring. The woman in the movie was so bored after a while. He had great information but it got to be too much. But with mysticism, you never feel it is too much. Hours and hours and hours of talking about ego and understanding of the self never becomes too much because it is the way of the moment, and the way of the moment makes the space very strong.

*"The past means
anything before this very moment…
and this one…
and this one…
and this one too."*

–Sharam

TRUST

"If Shahed's ego isn't accepted one hundred percent, then she doesn't trust that person."

SHAHED: There is something in me that doesn't like not knowing what is being said behind my back. For example, even now, I want to know what was the conversation that led to this quote being written down, I want to know. What is this part of the ego?

SHARAM: The ego wants to know what is behind something all the time. I told Nima—he always wants to know what is behind what people are saying. I told him for twenty-four hours not to worry about this "behind something" and come and report to me. He said, "Life becomes so easy, so wonderful. I actually stayed in the moment for twenty-four hours because I didn't worry about finding out what was behind something. I took things at face value and life became easier, I was happy." So we cut the hands of the ego when we don't want to know what is behind something. If I always need to know, I will be in misery all the time.

SHAHED: What makes the ego think there is something behind what people say?

SHARAM: Ego wants to act like God. It wants to know everything, but if it knows everything then we will be a mess. You come and sit in front of me and you say, "Hello Sharam, my name is Shahed." I say "Hi." In that first look, I know everything about you, but I see that there are some things I can share with you now and some things I need to wait to tell you. Maybe I even need to wait ten years to tell you. Something else needs twelve more years. I can't tell you everything right now.

Then the ego says, "Why don't you tell me everything now, you are hiding something from me." Of course I'm hiding something from you, because you are not ready to hear something that needs to be said ten years down the line.

SHAHED: Is this quote at the beginning true about where my trust issues come from?

SHARAM: If Shahed's ego isn't accepted one hundred percent then she doesn't trust that person. I think this is the most beautiful thing. This is about every ego. The ego has to be accepted one hundred percent, otherwise it doesn't trust. Here *(with Sharam)*, we are reducing the ego by bringing understanding; so the ego has been reduced. You guys, if you still had the egos that you started with, with me, you wouldn't be able to stand each other *(lots of laughter)*. Now your acceptance level, your love, has increased because you understand. You are waking up daily *(your consciousness)* and the ego is losing ground daily.

SHAHED: I really want to trust you fully, but my ego doesn't want to trust you.

SHARAM: But that's the job of ego, not wanting to trust. If I don't accept you one hundred percent, then you don't trust me. You see, for example, the book becomes part of your ego. Because we think we are the ego, or the book, so if somebody doesn't like the book, they don't like you.

SHAHED: Why does the ego get so invested in people liking us? Why do we even develop that way?

SHARAM: The reason we are so attached to things and the ego is that we have been taught.... You see, everything is the mind, which is a castle that is made out of cards, or imagination. In our mind, we have been taught that we are being attacked by someone outside all the time. People are there to attack you. Everybody is ultimately cruel, and we better watch out because they are out to get us. As a child, we've been taught not to trust, so we grow up and we don't trust. We are always wanting to see what the other person is going to do. We don't trust them; we are ready to hate them. It is just a learned thing from society, through our parents. People don't open up to one another. They are strangers.

SHAHED: It just feels so absolute, that if people don't like you, that there is nothing left. Why is that?

SHARAM: Because the ego doesn't believe that there is a soul. You think you are a book, or a house, or money. The ego doesn't know that we have a core.

SHAHED: Why is it so subtle?

SHARAM: Why is the soul so subtle? The soul says, "Who says I am subtle? I am also gross. Your grossness and your subtleness are both me. I am on the surface as much as I am in the depth."

But you forget the depth....

SHAHED: Is the soul the ego too?

SHARAM: (*Sharam using his hands to demonstrate*) The surface and the core, there is this much distance between the two (*see diagram next page*).

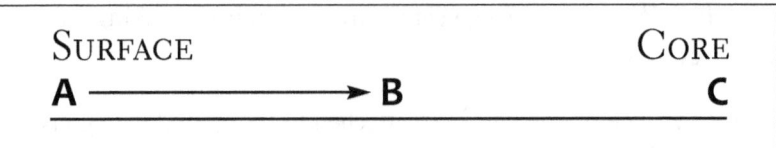

What is the ego? Ego is not getting to the core. You are walking to the core. You are here at point B. You started at A, now you're at point B. You understand this much (A to B), but you don't understand the rest (B to C). And if you don't know the core, we call that ego. But, you understand much more than you did. When you make that final jump to the core, when you get to C, then you have the core and the surface, and the whole distance in between. Then you see that you are so subtle, you don't get bothered anymore because you have the core with you. You have everything. Mysticism is all or nothing. If you have all, (A to C) you have everything, if you don't have all, then you have nothing. You just have ego. So we are really going fast to get to the core. We need the depth of the core to see everything. If we don't have that, if we just have this much (AB), then what we don't have (BC), we call ego. We don't have the depth of understanding. I see all the flaws in you. I see your passivity, your aggression, your being a kid. I could go on and on and on about your ego, but it would become just something in your mind. You haven't experienced it. You have to go step by step. Every day, we break a barrier, then move forward, until we reach the core. This is what we call gaining subtlety. Roxana said to me the other day, "The hardest thing to do is to become more subtle." She is right. It is hard, but not impossible, and remember, it is the only reason we are here on Earth.

A "Kshhh" and a "Fshhh"

SHAHED: I really want to trust you fully, but my ego doesn't want to trust you.

SHARAM: But that's the job of ego, not wanting to trust. If I don't respect your ego or if I don't accept you one hundred percent, then you don't trust me. You see, for example, the book becomes part of your ego. Because we think we are the ego, or the book, if somebody doesn't like the book then they don't like you. They don't respect you. This reminds me of a story:

> *Once Mullah Nasruddin and Donelle, his wife, were traveling through a village. When they got to the center of the village, they noticed that the people were making a huge pot of sparrow soup for everyone. Mullah walked over, pointed his hand towards the pot, and said "kshhh" (shoo) and all of the sudden, all the sparrows from the pot came back to life and flew away. The people were so amazed that they started following Mullah and his wife. They said, "This is a miracle. He is a saint." They followed them to the village's edge, where Mullah casually walked to the side of the road, turned his back on the people and started peeing. The people were so offended. They started cursing him and swearing at him. Donelle turned to Mullah and said, "Why did you do that?!! Everyone had such faith in you, why did you ruin it?"*
>
> *Mullah said, "The faith that comes with a 'kshhh' and goes with a 'fshhh' (the sound of peeing), we're better off without."*

SHARAM: So why is it better that the trust that comes from the ego goes away? Because every time that happens, really it is an opportunity for you to look at the ego even deeper. Then you gain more subtlety and understanding of it.

THE MECHANICS OF WATCHING

As you know from reading these sittings, we (Sharam's students) usually talk to him about the parts of ourselves or others that we don't like, that we condemn, the parts we want to get rid of. Invariably he tells us not to try to change these things—don't try to not be angry, just watch the anger when it comes up, and keep watching and eventually it will go away on its own.)

SHARAM: Watching something implies trying to get rid of it. To try to get rid of something means, first, censoring that thing. We are watching with the intention to get rid of. Therefore, there is a division. There is something we want to separate ourselves from. We learned that watching something makes it stronger, so that you can see it. We want to get rid of something, for example anger, by watching it. Then, that thing becomes stronger. So by watching, you may think things are becoming worse. Yes, things are getting worse, but they are getting worse to get better.

Someone's path is love. Love gives you eyes to see things with deep acceptance, not to get rid of them. You just see things and they go away by themselves. It's amazing when you feel this deep connection with me, you feel the love and the love gives you eyes to see. You just simply see things and know that they will be gone. It's amazing that with love, you don't *need* to see. You just see anyway. Meditation will do that too. So when you are meditating or loving, you gain eyes.

QUESTION: Can you repeat that please?

SHARAM: If we are watching, for example, our anger, because we want to get rid of it, it only gets bigger. It resists more. The bigger it gets, the easier it is to see. But if you simply gain eyes, you see the flaws in you, just by themselves, not with the motivation of getting rid of them, and they go away. You are not negating anything, you have simply gained eyes to better see, through love and deep meditation. That's all.

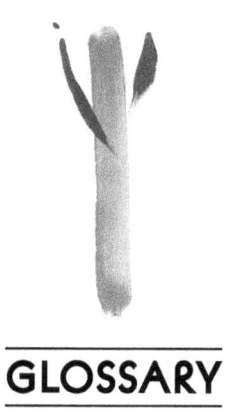

GLOSSARY

AWARENESS: In normal life, we usually are not aware of our Being. We only associate ourselves with our thoughts. Awareness means becoming aware of our being by stopping the mind. We can stop the mind with meditation, focusing, or experiencing a moment of deep joy or understanding.

BODIES OF THE SOUL: We humans have seven different layers in our soul. We call them the bodies of the soul. The physical body is at the center of these layers, while all the other bodies move outwards from this center like the ripples created by throwing a stone in a lake.

> **FIRST BODY: Physical Body**
>
> **SECOND BODY: Etheric Body** – The etheric body extends about one inch beyond our physical body. All the chakras are part of this body.
>
> **THIRD BODY: Emotional Body** – The emotional body extends about three feet out from the physical body. It is the body that stores our emotions.
>
> **FOURTH BODY: Mental Body** – The mental body extends beyond the emotional body, but the extent to which it and the rest

of the bodies do so depends upon our spiritual advancement. The mental body carries our thoughts and relates to the mind.

FIFTH BODY: Bliss Body – Where ecstasy resides. Contains the information of the past. Hearing the voice of Existence.

SIXTH BODY: Spiritual Body – Contains the information of the future. Seeing the Beyond.

SEVENTH BODY: Universal Body – Joining with the universe. Becoming one with God.

CHAKRAS: The chakras are centers of the soul. They sit in the spine and head and direct different aspects of being.

FIRST CHAKRA: The first chakra is primarily concerned with survival issues, money, the instinctual. The way the first chakra operates is through attachment.

SECOND CHAKRA: The second chakra is more about pleasure, sex, and the emotions.

THIRD CHAKRA: Relates to power, control, and the mental body, the mind.

FOURTH CHAKRA: The heart center concerned with trust, letting go, love and acceptance.

FIFTH CHAKRA: Involved in expressing and hearing: specifically hearing the voice of Existence.

SIXTH CHAKRA: The sixth chakra is also called the third eye which sees the hidden aspects of Existence, aspects the other five senses cannot sense.

SEVENTH CHAKRA: Relates to dropping attachments to the material world totally. Living in the divine with absolute freedom.

CLEANSING: Getting rid of the energies that are not subtle (karma) and are blocking our chakras, causing us emotional pain, discomfort, and misery.

CONCENTRATION: Means focusing. Sometimes meditation and concentration get confused. Concentration is the first step to meditation. We use the mind to beat the mind by focusing totally. When we focus totally, we use the mind intensively, so much so that all of a sudden, it stops and meditation happens.

CONDITIONING: Teachings from our parents, teachers, and the society in general, that create our belief systems and personality.

CONSCIOUSNESS: The mind is divided into two parts: the part we are aware of called consciousness, and a much larger part of which we are not aware, the sub- or unconscious. The subconscious controls much of our feelings and reactions automatically, without our really understanding why.

ECSTACY: A state of being where all the darkness of the soul is gone, leaving tremendous satisfaction or joy. Enlightenment is a state of everlasting ecstacy.

ENLIGHTENMENT: Simply put, the individual is in charge of, or has conquered his ego and is in direct contact with Existence. His consciousness is lit up.

EXISTENCE: Existence includes everything in the universe from the material, animal, and the human to the emotional, mental, energetic … everything. We use this term almost synonymously with God, except that we are not separate from Existence. We are a necessary and vital part of the whole. It includes the deepest levels of understanding to the most shallow, and includes all aspects of human behavior, regardless of how we judge these behaviors as good or bad, valuable or not valuable. All is essential to the whole.

GOING TO THE HEART: Being in the heart or going to the heart means our kundalini energy rises from the first chakra up through the spine, passing all the lower chakras as it goes. As we travel higher up this main artery of the soul, the pathways become more subtle. So the energy can only continue to climb based on how subtle it has become. When we are stuck in the lower chakras, we feel that we are not safe enough. We believe that we need to control the things around us. To do this we use the mind. A lot of energy is used by the mind for thinking, which causes emotional pain, unhappiness, and a feeling of heaviness. Feeling love is the key to making the energy subtle enough to climb to the heart chakra and higher, which brings feelings of love, gentleness, and let-go. This is what we call going to the heart.

KARMA: Karma is a negative energy that creates blockages in the soul and the body.

KUNDALINI: The source of our personal energy, sitting in the first chakra. Also called the energy of our life or the energy of the soul.

MALE/FEMALE: The kundalini energy is broken into two parts, male and female, regardless of whether you are a man or a woman. The left side of the body is governed by the female energy and the right side is governed by the male.

MEDITATION: State of no mind, but when we talk about meditation, mostly it means creating situations to help the mind to stop, like sitting in silence and closing the eyes.

PRANA: The energy of Existence that we take in from our surroundings by breathing, eating, etc.

SUBCONSCIOUS (UNCONSCIOUS): Subconscious is below the conscious. Many paths divide the subconscious into subconscious and unconscious, but for general understanding, subconscious and unconscious are the same thing, unless you want to dissect them for different points of understanding. For example, subconscious is the new material that has been put in the basement of our mind. Unconscious is the older material, even from our last lifetime.

TOTALITY: Becoming as intense, as completely focused as possible, in whatever we are doing or feeling.

TRANSFORMATION: Transformation is when the mind stops, for whatever reason, and in result some blockages open up. Deep understanding will cause the mind to step aside. The ego also steps aside when the mind stops and our kundalini energy moves to the heart or higher, allowing for deep peace, joy, and ecstasy. Consequently, we experience inner opening and change.

www.ingramcontent.com/pod-product-compliance
Lightning Source LLC
Chambersburg PA
CBHW071651090426
42738CB00009B/1489